SUMMARY GUIDES

ENGLISH

Kate McGregor

First published in 2025 by Insight Publications

Insight Publications Pty Ltd
3/350 Charman Road
Cheltenham VIC 3192
Australia

Tel: +61 3 8571 4950
Email: books@insightpublications.com.au

www.insightpublications.com.au

Summary Guides English 7 / Kate McGregor

Kate McGregor asserts the moral right to be identified as the author of this work.

ISBN: 9781923154124 (print)

Publisher: Kate McGregor
Copy editors: Leanne Peters, Naomi Saligari
Proofreaders: Alison Tealby, Robert Beardwood, Olivia Shenken
Cover and text designer: Melisa Paredes
Typesetter: Aptara®, Inc.
Printed by Markono Print Media Pte Ltd.

Insight Publications acknowledges the Traditional Custodians of the Country on which we meet and work, the Boonwurrung People of the Kulin Nation. We pay our respects to Elders past and present, and extend that respect to all Aboriginal and Torres Strait Islander peoples.

Please be aware this book contains names of Aboriginal and Torres Strait Islander people who may be deceased.

Contents

PART 3: LITERACY 93

Introduction

What you learn in English is guided by a document called a **curriculum**. This book blends the Australian and state curricula to summarise what you need to know in Year 7.

It will help you understand the different types of English texts and teach you the skills to create your own stories, essays and presentations.

The book is separated into three parts: language, literature and literacy. These are the three key strands for learning English.

Key term

curriculum: the subjects studied in a course, and what each subject includes

Language, literature and literacy explained

Isn't English just English? Well, yes, but you can break it up into different things to focus on – like the strands in a rope.

- **Language** is about the skills you need to communicate. It's the how: How do I explain myself clearly? How do I organise my writing to make it clear? How do I know which words will fit best in different situations?
- **Literature** is about looking at different kinds of writing and analysing how they work. How does the way a poem is written make you feel something? How has an author made their story feel exciting?
- **Literacy** refers to the ability to read and write. These are specific skills within the broader concept of a language. Literacy involves understanding written texts, decoding words and composing messages. Literacy focuses specifically on the skills you need to engage with the written and spoken word.

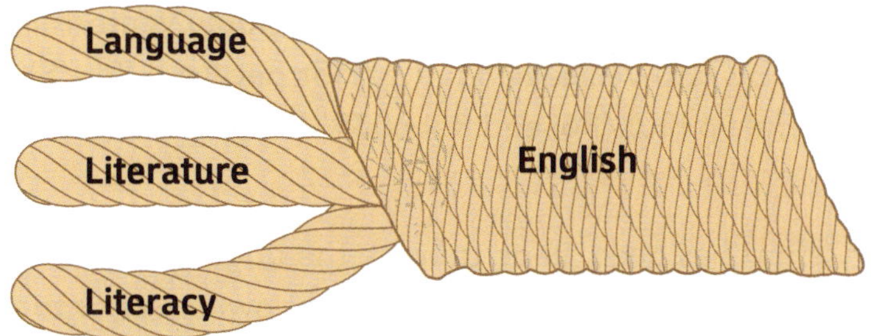

The three strands of English

Answers

Go to www.insightpublications.com.au/resources for selected answers to the activities.

Acknowledgements

The authors of *Summary Guides English 7* thank the following writers for their contributions: Robert Beardwood, Anica Boulanger-Mashberg, Charlotte Long, Melanie Napthine and Olivia Shenken.

Insight Publications is grateful to the following individuals and organisations for permission to reproduce copyright material.

Text

Extract by Aditya Joshi from *The Conversation*, 29 July 2025, '"Are you joking, mate?" AI doesn't get sarcasm in non-American varieties of English', CC BY 4.0 p.13; extract by Phoebe Hart from *The Conversation*, 1 July 2025, 'What to watch in July: KPop Demon Hunters', CC BY 4.0 pp.20–1; extract by Megan Carrigy from *The Conversation*, 10 November 2021, 'The Drover's Wife: the Legend of Molly Johnson brings a Black woman's perspective to Australian frontier films', CC BY 4.0 pp.58–9; Ruari Jack Hughes, 'The City and the City', first published in *Cordite Poetry Review*, 2024 pp.60–1; extract by Felicity Meakins from *The Conversation*, 8 May 2015, 'Some Australian Indigenous languages you should know', CC BY 4.0 pp.123–4

Images

Alamy/©Samuel Goldwyn Films/Courtesy Everett Collection p.59; Shutterstock/ Aleksandr Lysenko p.2, /GoodStudio p.5, /Anastasia Boiko p.7, /Mila Basenko p.8, /LookerStudio p.9, /Bibadash p.12, /TA Design p.14, /MITstudio p.22, /Lana Sham p.26, /GoodStudio p.30, /Max Morphine p.35, /The Studio p.38, /Microstocker.Pro p.40, /Juca B p.44, /Prostock-studio p.45 top left, /Lykos Productions p.45 top right, /Studio Romantic p.45 2nd row left, /Kirayonak Yuliya p.45 2nd row right, /Xavier Lorenzo p.45 3rd row left, /Gorodenkoff p.45 3rd row right, /noomcpk 4th row left, /Denis_Komarov p.45 4th row right, /Alex Jackson p.45 bottom row left, /PLCNSK p.45 bottom row right, /upsidesmile p.47, /Miles Clifford Triniman p.53, /Tomacco p.55, /Roman Samborskyi p.64, /Vectorbum p.66, /breakermaximus p.69, /Aditia fidiantoro p.78, /wavebreakmedia p.97, /Nadya_Art p.100, /VectorMine p.107, / Ghariza Mahavira p.115, /Tero Vesalainen p.117, /HStrongArt p.121, /SK_Sabbir p.126, /svekloid p.129, /LineTale p.130, /Roi and Roi p.139, /Lamai Prasitsuwan p.140, /lala firdaa p.142

PART 1 LANGUAGE

Using language to express yourself and interact with others

1.1 Language and identity

The main reason we study English is to communicate: to express ourselves, share our ideas and interact with others. We develop our language skills so we can say exactly what we mean and can understand what others are saying to us.

What is your identity?

A person's identity is their sense of self – their concept of who they are. Using language is a powerful way to express your identity.

Think about it

What do you mean when you talk about your identity? What kind of adjectives (describing words) do you use to say who you are? For example, young, sporty, studious, funny, rebellious or easy-going.

Sometimes we define who we are by talking about our values, which are the things we believe are important. What are some of your values? For example, is being kind or brave important to you? Do you care about how someone treats others?

Most people have a personal identity and a social identity.

Personal identity

An individual's personal identity, or sense of who they are, comes from their distinct features and characteristics. Table 1.1 shows four fundamental elements of personal identity.

Table 1.1: Personal identity elements

Demographics (e.g. specific population groups you belong to)	Gender, age and ethnicity
Psychological traits	Personality, beliefs and values
Physical attributes	Size, sense of style, general appearance
Cultural ties	Language, traditions and customs

These four elements work together to create a unique personal story that separates one person from another. Each element helps shape how a person views themselves and navigates their interactions with others.

We are so much more than what is on our student ID card. How do we express that creatively?

Social identity

A person's social identity relates to the social groups they belong to. Most people belong to many social groups. We usually share some characteristics or situations with some of the people in these groups.

Some social groups are shown in the diagram below. Your social identity may also include other people you have things in common with such as those of a similar age, gender, class or sexuality.

Social groups form part of your social identity.

Activity 1.1.1

1 Fill in the table below to explain your personal identity.

Demographics	
Psychological traits	
Physical attributes	
Cultural ties	

2 Write one or two sentences that explain your social identity.

How to express a character's identity

Writers of fictional texts express the personal and social identities of their characters in many ways, including through their names, the style of language they use, how they look (appearance) and what they do (actions).

Names

The names of characters in fictional texts can provide clues about who they are. For example, the character name Severus Snape has several **connotations** that give us more information about this character.

- 'Severus' means strict, stern and severe in Latin, which suits this character's behaviour towards his students.
- Septimius Severus was a great Roman emperor, perhaps implying the greatness of the character.
- 'To sever' means to cut, which implies that someone with the name Severus is dangerous.

Key term

connotation: an implied or associated meaning; an idea or feeling that a word evokes for a person in addition to its intended or primary meaning

Fun fact

Authors often use distinctive names as a shortcut to tell us about a character. They can also use more common names as a way to, for example, add realism.

The character of James Bond has that name because the author wanted something that wouldn't stand out. However, the name is now iconic because of the character!

A real-life example of a person's name reflecting their identity is Oodgeroo Noonuccal. Noonuccal is one of Australia's most influential First Nations writers, who devoted her life to telling the stories of First Nations peoples – in poetry, in visual art, through a rich oral tradition, and as an activist. Noonuccal was named Kathleen Jean Mary Ruska when she was born in 1920. In 1988, she changed her name to Oodgeroo ('paperbark tree') Noonuccal (after her ancestors and home) to reflect her Aboriginal identity.

Language

Similarly, the language characters use (in their speech and thoughts) can provide clues about who they are. For example, a character says, 'Crikey mate, it's so hot,

I gotta get outta here. I'll see ya later this arvo for a potato scallop'. This short piece of **dialogue** gives us lots of information about this character. They are using an informal version of Australian English that many Australians use in everyday conversations – so they are probably Australian.

In this piece of dialogue, we can see some of the features of Australian English: abbreviating (shortening) words and using **contractions** and **elisions**. You could say that using abbreviations, contractions and elisions, particularly when speaking to each other, is part of our Australian social identity.

Key terms

dialogue: conversation between characters

contraction: an abbreviated version of a word or words, formed by shortening a word or merging two words into one (e.g. 'do not' becomes 'don't')

elision: where two or more spoken words run together (e.g. 'got to' becomes 'gotta')

Also, in the piece of dialogue above, the character has called a 'potato cake' a 'potato scallop', which tells us they're likely from Queensland, New South Wales or Western Australia. When you say the dialogue aloud, you can also hear that the character has a broad Australian accent, which is more commonly heard in rural rather than metropolitan areas. (For information about the rules of writing dialogue, see 'How to punctuate dialogue' on page 6).

Another way language can show identity is through a person's use of idiom.

Understanding idioms

Have you ever 'bitten someone's head off'? You didn't actually bite someone, did you? Instead, you snapped at them angrily. This is an example of an idiom.

Idioms are a type of **figurative language**. These are phrases that are used in a non-literal way for effect; the words don't mean what they usually mean. For example, when you 'open a can of worms', you are not actually opening a can that is filled with worms! Instead, this phrase means you are starting something that will probably be complicated or difficult.

Idioms are specific to a language. That means that an idiom in one language does not necessarily makes sense in another language. For example, the Spanish idiom '*ahogarse en un vaso de agua*' means 'to drown yourself in a glass of water' in English. But its actual meaning is to make a problem bigger than it is. In English, we have our own idiom about making a problem bigger than it is: 'To make a mountain out of a molehill'.

Therefore, using Australian idioms is also a way to express our Australian social identity.

Appearance

Writers of fictional texts also express the personal and social identities of their characters by describing what they look like. Good writers avoid providing details that don't tell the reader anything about who the characters are. It is better to think of and include unique or unusual details that provide clues about a character's identity.

For example, it may not matter whether a main character has blonde, brown or black hair. Instead, maybe the main character's head is shaved in unusual patches. This tells the reader that something out of the ordinary may have happened that connects to the main character's identity. Have they shaved their head to raise money for a cause or as part of a dare? Why would it be patchy? How do the people in the main character's social groups react when they notice the unusual feature?

Similarly, describing a character's clothes can give the reader an idea of the personal or social identity of a particular character, but you don't need to go into detail about every item a person has on! Instead, pick one or two elements that tell the reader something important about your character. Don't forget to use descriptive language!

Use appearance to provide clues about a character's personal and social identity.

Actions

How a character acts or what they do gives us a huge insight into their identity. For a real-life example, many politicians say they care about young people. But if you check what they have done while in government, their actions may tell a different story.

 Activity 1.1.2

1 Look up your name. Does it have any connotations? Do these align with your sense of self?

2 Pretend you are a character in a novel. Write a paragraph expressing the personal and social identities of you as a character. Avoid writing in the first person (I, me) and instead use the third person (she, he, they). Use dialogue and descriptions of your appearance and actions to express who you are.

3 Consider the Australian idiom: 'Put a sock in it!' What is the figurative meaning of this phrase?

How to punctuate dialogue

Dialogue (also called **direct speech**) is an important part of many fictional texts. Not only can readers learn a lot about characters from what they say and how they speak, but dialogue can also help move the plot forward by communicating events and conflicts in interesting and engaging ways.

Dialogue is often accompanied by dialogue tags; these are phrases that indicate who is speaking (e.g. 'he said', 'she said').

Follow these rules to punctuate the dialogue in the texts you write:

- Use quotation marks (' ') to enclose spoken words.
- Start a new line each time a different person speaks.
- Separate dialogue from dialogue tags with commas or full stops.
- Place punctuation within the quotation marks.
- Break up the dialogue with action.
- Use the dialogue tags before, in the middle of, or after the dialogue
- Leave out the dialogue tag if it is clear who is speaking.

Look at Table 1.2 to see these rules put into practice.

Table 1.2: Punctuating dialogue

Sample text	Explanation
'I can't believe she did that,' Tran said.	Place the dialogue inside the quotation marks. Use a comma or full stop to separate what is being said from the dialogue tag.
'Did what?' Bailey asked.	Place the punctuation inside the quotation marks.
Tran watched as Amanda retreated into the distance.	Use action to break up the dialogue.
'She just killed it, without feeling!' said Tran. 'It may be a bug but it's still a living thing!'	Dialogue tags can go before, in the middle of, or after dialogue.
'You've always been a softie, Tran. It's just a bug. Don't stress about it.'	Not every piece of dialogue needs a dialogue tag; if it is clear who is speaking, leave out the tag.

Key fact

When it comes to dialogue tags, 'said' is usually best. Sometimes students are encouraged to have their characters yelp, exclaim or gasp their words instead. While these terms can make your writing interesting, too many can be distracting, so use them with care.

Activity 1.1.3

1 **Add correct punctuation to the following sentences.**

  a **What's for dinner, Mum? I yelled I'm starving.**

  b **That was way too close Kate said as the motorbike whizzed past.**

  c **Malia asked can you help me with this?**

2 **Write a conversation between two characters or a real conversation that you had with a friend. Break up the conversation with some action. Once you are finished, check that you have included the correct punctuation.**

How to use dialogue in comics, cartoons and animations

Let's look at how the creators of **comics**, **cartoons** and **animations** use dialogue to show the audience who the characters are. These text types all use visual storytelling, where images and text work together to set the scene, develop characters and advance the plot. Often, in these types of texts, a lot of the text is dialogue.

Dialogue plays a crucial role in visual storytelling.

Key terms

comic: a magazine or book where the story is told in pictures with a small amount of writing; often presented as a series of sequential panels (e.g. *The Amazing Spider-Man*)

cartoon: a simple drawing where the subject or situation is depicted in an exaggerated way; usually humorous; intended as a comment on something (e.g. a cartoon in a newspaper)

animation: a way of making a movie or video game by using a series of drawings, computer graphics or photographs of objects (e.g. *Spider-Man: Into the Spider-Verse*)

In these text types, the use of visual cues such as facial expressions, body language and panel layout complements the dialogue and enhances characterisation.

The following guidelines will help you use dialogue in comics, cartoons and animation effectively.

- **Keep it short:** You have a limited amount of space, so every word has to be there for a reason (i.e. to reveal something about a character or drive the story forward)
- **Say it in the artwork:** Save your dialogue for things that you can't communicate visually. For example, don't have your character say they are upset, when you can draw them with a sad face.

- **Break it up:** In comics, break conversations into different panels depending on what you want to focus on and how you want a scene to flow.
- **Use authentic dialogue:** The dialogue of a character should sound natural (i.e. it uses real-life speech patterns) and authentic (i.e. it sounds like something the character would say). For example, an evil professor should speak differently to a kid in primary school. (This advice works for prose storytelling too!)
- **Vary rhythm and tone:** In comics, avoid using the same amount of text in every panel and instead play around with what and how much you include. Don't forget to use silence, too. Using a variety of approaches to your dialogue keeps things interesting.

Key term

tone: the emotion or attitude expressed in a text or image

Activity 1.1.4

1 Add dialogue to the comic below.

a What is the grey-haired man saying? What does this tell us about him?

b Do the shadowy figures have anything to say?

c Look at the woman with her hand raised. What question is she asking? What does this tell us about her?

2 Create your own page of a graphic novel. Use dialogue to show the reader who your characters are.

1.2 How to write an evaluation

What is an evaluation?

To **evaluate** means to assess the worth of something. An evaluation of a text looks at the different elements of that text and considers how well they contribute to the text achieving its **purpose**.

Key terms

evaluate: to judge, appraise or review something; an evaluation uses language to express feelings and opinions, make judgements, and assess the quality of ideas and features of texts

purpose: the reason for a text being written; the writer's or speaker's desired outcome (e.g. to entertain, inform, or convince the audience of a point of view)

Language used to evaluate texts

In English, when we evaluate something, we use specific language called **evaluative language**. Some examples of evaluative language are included in Table 1.3 below.

Table 1.3: Examples of evaluative language

good	effective	tedious	impressive	superficial
outstanding	disappointing	fair	fascinating	unoriginal
inspiring	moving	acceptable	uninteresting	fresh
upsetting	adequate	incredible	clear	engaging

Key term

evaluative language: positive, neutral or negative language that judges the worth of something; it expresses feelings and opinions, makes judgements, and assesses the quality of ideas and features of texts

We can also use evaluative language to show the extent of similarity or difference between one thing and another. Table 1.4 on the next page gives some examples.

Table 1.4: Evaluative language showing the extent of similarity or difference between things

Minor difference	somewhat	marginal	negligible	subtle	slight
Major difference	large	extensive	considerable	significant	vast

Activity 1.2.1

1 **Sort the evaluative words in Table 1.3 into lists of positive, neutral and negative words. Then add three words of your own to each list.**

2 **Highlight the evaluative language used in the short film review below.**

> 'This excellent movie features an impressive number of shots filmed with a handheld camera. This interesting filming style helped me to feel much closer to the action that was happening on the screen. This made the movie far more entertaining'.

3 **Think about a book you have read or a movie or TV show you have watched. How would you evaluate the experience? Write three sentences: in the first sentence, evaluate if it was too long or short; in the second sentence, judge if it was exciting enough; in the third sentence, explain what you thought of the main characters.**

How to substantiate an evaluation

When evaluating a text, you need to **substantiate** your claims. This means providing reasons and evidence to support your judgement of an element of a text.

People can struggle to provide reasons for how they feel about something: when you chat with friends, someone might say, 'I hate that movie' but if you ask why, they often say, 'Dunno, I just do'. Unfortunately, this information doesn't necessarily help you decide if you want to watch the movie or avoid it! However, if they provide reasons for their **opinion**, you will have a better idea of whether you would enjoy the movie. For example, if they say, 'I thought it dragged, and I didn't think the main character was very believable', then you can use that information to make an informed decision.

As well as backing up what you say with reasons, it is also important to provide **evidence** (direct quotes) from the text to support your opinions. Supporting your arguments with evidence is an excellent way to give your evaluation credibility and show that you understand the text you are assessing.

Key terms

substantiate: to use evidence to support a claim or argument

opinions: personal thoughts and feelings on a topic including, when studying English, subjective and personal responses to a text

Understanding direct quotes

Using direct quotes from the text to support your arguments means using the actual words from the text. Using direct quotes, and integrating them into your writing, can improve the quality of your analysis. We can show this with three examples below, showing different levels of evaluation:

- **Basic evaluation:** The villain in the book was too cartoonish, so I didn't find her believable. The things she said were a bit over the top. (No quotes included.)
- **Mid-range evaluation:** The villain in the book was too cartoonish, saying things like 'Fools! I'll get you next time!' and 'Gah! Vanquished again!' I found this made her less believable, especially because the rest of the story is written in a realistic style. (Quotes are included but have not been integrated with the text.)
- **High-quality evaluation:** The story uses realism to heighten our engagement with the characters. However, this is undermined by the villain's somewhat cartoonish language. As she yowls about being 'vanquished' and shakes her fist at 'fools' who she will 'get next time!', we are almost pulled out of the realistic setting and into another film, which feels jarring. (Quotes are integrated with the text – note that this is quite advanced for Year 7 English!)

Avoid quoting whole paragraphs of text. Your goal is to use the quotes to substantiate what *you* say, not to repeat what someone else says.

Activity 1.2.2

Write one or two paragraphs evaluating a book you have read or a show you have watched. Substantiate your opinion with evidence.

Evaluating different text types

For this section, it may be helpful to refer to Table 1.5: The structure and purpose of some text types (page 15). Remember that when evaluating a text, you must consider how well its different elements contribute to the text achieving its purpose.

How to evaluate narrative texts

In general, the purpose of a narrative text is to tell a story. Authors of narrative texts usually want to entertain their readers. Many authors also try to teach lessons, convey information (e.g. about a particular time, place or event in history) and explore **themes** in their stories.

Key term

theme: the 'big ideas' explored in a story (e.g. love, power, good versus evil, family, friendship, sacrifice); most authors won't tell you the themes of their story directly – readers have to work them out for themselves

Here are some elements of a narrative text that you can examine in an evaluation.

- **The plot:** Does the story make sense? Is it interesting? What information, lessons or themes does the plot convey?
- **The characters:** Are the characters believable? Do you know too much or too little about them? What do the characters add to the information, lessons or themes the story is conveying? (Think about what the characters do and say.)
- **The setting:** Are the time and place of the story portrayed convincingly? Are there any parts of the setting that seem odd or out of place? What era is the story set? How does the setting contribute to the information, lessons or themes conveyed in the story?
- **The writing:** Is the language used descriptive or matter-of-fact? Is the writing style fast paced or thoughtful?

When you evaluate a character, you need to consider how that character contributes to the text achieving its purpose.

Activity 1.2.3

1 Think of a character you found believable in a show you have watched or a book you have read. Identify three things that made them feel like a real person.

2 Identify three themes in a movie or show you have watched (e.g. what it means to be brave, the importance of friends, or the destructive power of revenge). How successfully do you think the creator explores these three themes?

How to evaluate persuasive texts

The purpose of a persuasive text is to convince the reader of a point of view.

Here are some elements of a persuasive text that you can examine in an evaluation.

- **The author's stance on an issue:** Is it clear what the author's opinion is? Could the author's position on a topic be misunderstood?
- **Their evidence:** Many persuasive texts include facts, statistics and quotes from reputable people to support the writer's point of view. Are these facts, statistics and quotes convincing?

- **The language:** Is the writing clear and easy to understand? Has the writer used **jargon**? Does this use of unfamiliar words make the text more or less convincing? (Later in the book, we will look at some of the persuasive devices authors use, such as repetition, the rule of three and appeals to fear, among others.)
- **The place of publication:** Where has the persuasive text been published? If it has been published in a well-regarded newspaper or journal, this adds credibility, as the article has probably been fact-checked. If the text has been self-published on a blog, it is less credible.

Key term

jargon: language particular to a trade, profession or other group

Read the persuasive text below.

'Are you joking, mate?' AI doesn't get sarcasm in non-American varieties of English

By Aditya Joshi, Senior Lecturer,
School of Computer Science and Engineering, UNSW Sydney

In 2018, my Australian co-worker asked me, 'Hey, how are you going?' My response – 'I am taking a bus' – was met with a smirk. I had recently moved to Australia. Despite studying English for more than 20 years, it took me a while to familiarise myself with the Australian variety of the language.

It turns out large language models powered by artificial intelligence (AI) such as ChatGPT experience a similar problem.

In new research, published in the *Findings of the Association for Computational Linguistics 2025*, my colleagues and I introduce a new tool for evaluating the ability of different large language models to detect sentiment and sarcasm in three varieties of English: Australian English, Indian English and British English.

The results show there is still a long way to go until the promised benefits of AI are enjoyed by all, no matter the type or variety of language they speak.

The Conversation, 29 July 2025

Activity 1.2.4

1. **Do you agree with what the author is saying in the persuasive text above? Why or why not?**
2. **Misinformation being published on the internet is becoming an increasingly serious issue. Brainstorm some ways creators on social media try to persuade people to agree with their point of view. How can you assess whether these authors are credible?**

1.3 How to organise a written text

One of the biggest things we are told in Year 7 is we have to get organised! In English, organising a text means using a clear, logical **structure**. A text's structure is the way an author has organised the information and ideas in the work; it is the overarching framework of the text.

Using a clear, logical structure in your writing will help ensure that the order of the information and ideas makes sense. This is called **sequencing**. A clear structure also helps readers understand the relationship between your ideas and helps them to follow your text as a whole.

Most texts have **structural elements**, which are parts of the text that contribute to its overall framework. For example, a poem may be structured as a sonnet, which has a certain number of lines and a certain number of syllables in each line.

Key terms

structure: the framework of a text; how the ideas and information are organised

sequencing: organising your ideas in a logical order, so they flow coherently from one to the next

structural elements: elements in a text that contribute to the overall form or framework of that text

The structure of a text depends on its purpose. The author's purpose influences how they organise the material in their text (i.e. how they structure it). The structure and purpose of some text types are listed in Table 1.5 on the next page.

Structuring and sequencing makes your text easier to follow.

Table 1.5: The structure and purpose of some text types

Text type	Examples	Purpose	Structure/structural elements
Narrative texts	Fiction (short stories, novels, graphic novels), narrative nonfiction	Tell a story	Often sequence the events of the plot in chronological order; use sections or chapters
Poetry	Haiku, sonnet, ballad, limerick, blank verse, epigram	Express feelings and ideas	Stanzas, number of lines, number of syllables in each line, and rhyme
Informative (expository) texts	Nonfiction such as news articles, essays, reviews, textbooks	Inform the audience about a topic	Usually use a simple structure (e.g. chapters with headings, introduction, main text, conclusion)
Persuasive texts	Opinion articles, advertisements, political speeches	Convince the audience of a point of view	Open with a particular position on an issue, introduce evidence to support that position, then summarise arguments
Procedural (instructional) texts	Recipes, how-to guides, manuals	Explain how to do something	Begin with a goal, followed by a list of materials, then finishes with steps in order

In Chapter 10, we will look at more complex structures such as cause and effect. For now, understanding the different structures and purposes of different text types will help you to organise, develop and link ideas in your own texts.

Key term

chronological order: describing events or information in the sequence of earliest to latest; from the Greek word *chronos*, meaning time

Activity 1.3.1

Choose a book that you have been assigned to read as part of your Year 7 English class. What do you think the text's purpose is? Can you identify three structural elements in your text?

How to structure common text types

As the table above shows, different text types have different purposes, and therefore need to be structured differently. The following pages will explore the structures of some common text types.

How to structure poetry

The purpose of poetry is to express feelings and ideas. There are many different types of poetry, including the haiku, ode, sonnet, ballad, elegy, limerick, blank verse and epigram.

All poems use structural elements. When describing the structure of poetry, we use specialist language such as 'line', 'stanza' and 'refrain'. Read Table 1.6 to make sure you understand the meanings of some common terms used to describe the structure of poems.

Table 1.6: Terms used to describe the structure of poems

Term	Meaning
form	The way the words are placed on the page
line	Words put together to form a line in a poem, similar to a sentence
line break	Where a line ends; this can shape how a poem is read
metre or rhythm	The 'beat' in the poem, similar to beats in music
refrain	Where something is repeated, often for emphasis
rhyme	When two words have the same end sound
rhyming scheme	The rhyming pattern of a poem
stanza	Multiple lines that belong together, similar to a paragraph

Structuring poetry involves considering the elements in the table above; for example, how many lines there should be, how many syllables in each line, how many stanzas there should be, and whether certain words should rhyme.

Some types of poetry follow specific, strict structural rules; for example:

- a **haiku** always has three lines; there are five syllables in the first and third lines, and seven syllables in the second line
- a **limerick** always has five lines; the first, second and fifth lines rhyme with each other; the third and fourth lines are shorter than the others and rhyme with each other
- a **sonnet** always has 14 lines; each line has 10 syllables; many sonnets use iambic pentameter, where each line contains five pairs of unstressed and stressed syllables
- a **blank verse** poem has 10 syllables; the last words of the lines must not rhyme; blank verse poems use iambic pentameter.

When writing a poem, you can follow the structural rules for a type of poem or you can write it without a structure and then play around with it afterwards. Poets often revise their work multiple times to get it 'right'. Play around with your poem: What happens if you end a line a few words earlier or later? If you repeat an image or phrase? If you move the stanzas around? Poetry is often playful, so try to have fun with the words when you are writing.

Activity 1.3.2

Read the last three stanzas of the famous poem 'Do not go gentle into that good night' by Dylan Thomas. This poem follows a type of structure called a 'villanelle'. A villanelle has 19 lines broken into six stanzas. The first five stanzas have three lines and the final stanza has four lines.

1 **Look at the last word of each line. Highlight the seven words that rhyme with each other. In another colour, highlight the three words that rhyme with each other. How would you describe this rhyming pattern?**

2 **A villanelle also includes two different lines that are repeated, called refrains. Underline the refrains in the poem below. Write a sentence explaining why you think Thomas used repetition in this way.**

Do not go gentle into that good night

...

Wild men who caught and sang the sun in flight,
And learn, too late, they grieved it on its way,
Do not go gentle into that good night.

Grave men, near death, who see with blinding sight
Blind eyes could blaze like meteors and be gay,
Rage, rage against the dying of the light.

And you, my father, there on the sad height,
Curse, bless, me now with your fierce tears, I pray.
Do not go gentle into that good night.
Rage, rage against the dying of the light.

3 **In your notebook, write your own haiku, limerick or sonnet.**

Think about it

Many popular songs are like poetry set to music. Listen to the songs of US rapper Kendrick Lamar or Australian hip-hop artist Joelistics. Do you think their lyrics are similar to poetry?

As well as discussing themes like love, loss and identity, poems and song lyrics often highlight ideas around social justice such as racism, inequality and the need for activism. Do you think poetry and songs are better suited to this purpose than other text types?

How to structure fiction

In general, the purpose of fictional texts is to tell a story. Types of fiction can include short stories, novels and graphic novels.

The structure of a work of fiction is the framework that organises the different elements of the story (the main events, setting, characters and themes) into a narrative that makes sense and is enjoyable to read. There are many ways to arrange these elements in a work of fiction; three structures are explained in Table 1.7.

Table 1.7: Three different ways to structure fiction

Structure	Explanation
Linear	The events are told in chronological order (the order in which they occur); typically has a clear beginning, middle and end.
Nonlinear	The events are told out of chronological order (i.e. the story jumps between time periods); may start with the middle, then go back to the beginning.
Circular	The story begins and ends at the same point.

One way to describe the structure of a work of fiction is to talk about its **story arc**. Also called a narrative arc or a dramatic arc, a story arc is the pattern made by a story. A common story arc used in fiction follows the pattern shown in the figure below.

Key term

story arc: the progression of a story

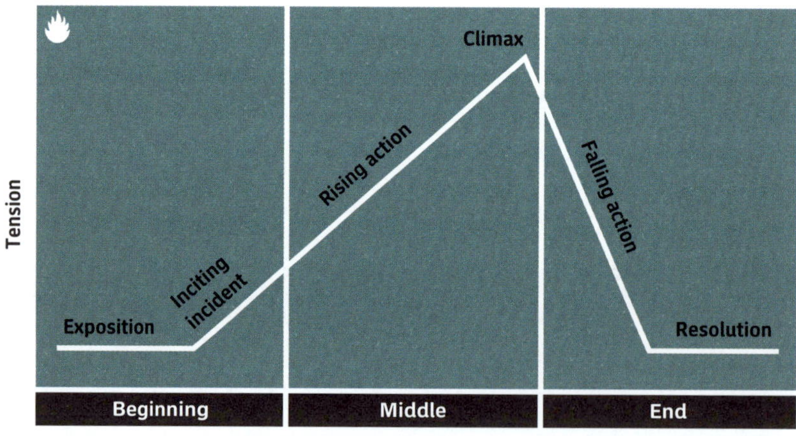

This diagram shows the story arc of a linear narrative; it indicates how the tension builds and recedes throughout the narrative.

Let's look at the elements of this diagram in more detail:

- **exposition:** an introduction that sets the scene by providing information about the key characters, the setting and any relevant background details
- **inciting incident:** something that happens and creates a problem or conflict for the main character

- **rising action:** a series of events that occur because of the problem or conflict; the rising action builds tension in the story
- **climax:** the turning point of a story where the action reaches its peak
- **falling action:** what happens after the climax; the consequences of the main character's actions become clear and the tension decreases
- **resolution:** where it is made clear how things have changed and the story is concluded.

Another way to arrange a story is to use the Kishōtenketsu structure. This is used in many classic Chinese, Korean, Vietnamese and Japanese narratives, including manga. This structure focuses on harmony and balance rather than on resolving a conflict. The Kishōtenketsu structure consists of four parts:

1. **Ki (introduction):** the story's scene is set
2. **Shō (development):** the story progresses and characters develop
3. **Ten (twist):** there is an unexpected turn that changes the direction of the story
4. **Ketsu (conclusion):** the story is resolved and any loose ends are tied up.

Narrative point of view

Another important part of the structure of fiction is the point of view of the narrator (the person telling the story); this is called 'narrative point of view'. Table 1.8 shows the different narrative points of view used in fiction.

Table 1.8: Narrative points of view used in fiction

Point of view	Explanation	Pronouns used	Example
First person	The story is told from the point of view of a character in the story.	I, me, my, mine	I looked up from the bottom of the vast canyon and felt so small. Was anybody looking for me?
Second person	The story is told as if the reader is a character in the story.	You, your, yours	You feel for a hold in the rock ledge. Your legs shake with tension. You wonder if you will survive.
Third person	The story is told by an external narrator who is not a character in the story themselves. This narrator is either omniscient or limited.	He, she, it, they, theirs	Abhi was worried she would lose sight of her friends. She called out, but they disappeared around a bend.

Key terms

third-person omniscient narrator: where the narrator has access to the thoughts and feelings of all the characters and all the facts related to the story

third-person limited narrator: where the narrator only has access to the thoughts and feelings of one character at a time

Activity 1.3.3

1 a **Write a plan for a story using the story arc structure shown in the diagram on page 18.**

b **Write the first paragraph of this story using the first-person narrative point of view.**

2 a **Write a plan for a story using the Kishōtenketsu structure.**

b **Write the first paragraph of this story using the third-person omniscient narrative point of view.**

3 **Research the 'save the cat' narrative structure. Write an explanation of this structure and show it to a classmate.**

How to structure nonfiction

The purpose of nonfiction texts is to inform readers about a topic. There are many different types of nonfiction texts, including textbooks, news articles, history books, academic essays, medical journal articles, biographies, books about travel and self-help books.

Many nonfiction texts use a simple structure: an **introduction** (provides an overview of what will be discussed), a **body** (a more detailed analysis and provides more information) and a **conclusion** (summarises the points made). These also often include the following structural elements: chapters, headings, block quotes and information presented in tables, graphs and diagrams.

Let's look at the structure of a film review in more detail. Film reviews describe the facts of a film's plot in simple terms (without spoilers!) (the introduction), then analyse some of the film's features (the body) and then evaluate the quality of the film (the conclusion). For example, read the following review of the animated movie *KPop Demon Hunters* by Phoebe Hart, Associate Professor, Film Screen & Animation, Queensland University of Technology.

> *KPop Demon Hunters* is an animated movie that follows a Korean girl band, Huntrix, whose members happen to be covert demon hunters. Their songs and slays have the power to maintain the barrier between the human world and the underworld (called the 'honmoon').
>
> Annoyed demon overlord Gwi-ma (voiced by Lee Byong-Hun) greenlights a devilishly sexy boy band, Saja Boys, to steal the girls' fans (and their souls). The

attack proves to be more than a challenge for lead singer, Rumi (Arden Cho), who has a dark secret she's keeping under wraps.

For fans of the Spider-Verse films, the animation style will be familiar: a blend of 2D and 3D techniques, with a high-contrast colour palette. *KPop Demon Hunters* goes an aesthetic step further by adding some distinctive anime touches, such as by using the chibi style, when characters have intense reactions.

The film also showcases several musical interludes voiced by actual K-pop stars such as EJAE, Kevin Woo, Andrew Choi and Rei Ami – as well as an anthem performed by members of TWICE, famous for their 2016 megahit Cheer Up.

To older viewers, the success of this watchable yet somewhat predictable flick may be puzzling, but *KPop Demon Hunters* will resonate with any Gen Zs in the house. After all, it has catchy tunes, jokes that land, female empowerment, epic battle scenes, and a smidge of teen romance.

There's also a deeper thematic [discussion] around the duality of identity, and a message about confronting one's own demons.

The Conversation, 1 July 2025

This example has a clear nonfiction structure. The author starts by describing what the film is about, then discusses the animation style and the music, both of which are vitally important to an animated film about KPop. Then, we move to the author's opinion of the film itself, which they describe as 'watchable yet somewhat predictable', along with a brief mention of its theme and message.

Activity 1.3.4

1 **Write a three-paragraph review of a book or show you have enjoyed. Pay attention to how you structure your review.**

2 **Challenge: Remember that a review is an evaluation. See if you can substantiate your evaluation with some quotes from the book or show.**

How to structure persuasive texts

The purpose of a persuasive text is to convince the audience of a point of view (that is, to get the reader to agree with the author's or speaker's opinion). The different types of persuasive texts include essays, advertisements, opinion articles and political speeches.

All persuasive texts feature a main argument (a contention). Some feature sub-arguments to provide reasons and extra evidence. Persuasive texts often include language features or techniques such as anecdotes (personal stories), emotive language, statistics and calls to action. For example, an influencer might tell an emotional story about how a product helped them (anecdote), then include some facts about the product (statistics), and then ask the viewer to buy the product (call to action).

The following image demonstrates some of the structural features of advertisements.

An advertisement for liquid yoghurt

The purpose of most advertising is to get you to buy a product or change a behaviour. The main argument for this product is that it is fresh and healthy, and therefore we should buy it! We can analyse the features used to make that argument.

Visually the image 'pops' with the bright white of the milk and the bottle standing out from the simple shaded background. There is repeated use of circles and curves, which draws the eye to the text and hints at the liquid and bubbling nature of the product. The images of cows support the idea of freshness – the milk is straight from the animal.

The text uses repetition, not only of phrases such as 'fresh' and 'freshly' but also of the statistics '0% fat' and '100% fresh milk'. The advertisement also uses technical terms – the circles contain 'LP33', 'GOS' and 'LGG', and seem to assume the viewer will know what these are (or perhaps we will just think they mean something healthy). The references to 'local farms', supporting 'the immune system' and being 'high in calcium' are meant to convince viewers that the product is good for them and the community. Overall, the advertisement appeals to people's desire for fresh and healthy food.

Note: Persuasive essays are also studied in Section 10.2 (pages 122–4). Advertisements are studied in more depth in Section 2.3 (pages 48–9).

Activity 1.3.5

1 There is a persuasive device called the 'rule of three', where things are listed in threes or mentioned three times. What is mentioned three times in the poster above?

2 There is no call to action on the poster above, such as 'buy now' or 'get one today'. Write a sentence saying why the poster should or should not include a call to action.

3 Create your own persuasive poster. Include some of the following elements: anecdote, statistics, emotive language and a call to action.

1.4 How to structure and sequence your writing

As discussed in Section 1.3, structure and sequencing help authors to communicate effectively. Structure and sequencing assist readers to understand an author's ideas and to follow the flow of events and ideas in a text.

In this section, we will learn about cohesion, which is a key element of any successfully structured and sequenced text. We will also explore connectives and signals: textual devices used to indicate structure and help your ideas flow logically.

What is cohesion?

A part of structure and sequence is **cohesion**. If a text is cohesive, it hangs together and makes sense as a whole. To create cohesion in a text, writers use textual devices such as connectives and repetition. These help to make connections between the ideas in a text and bind different parts of the text together, giving it a sense of unity.

Key term

cohesion: the action or fact of forming a united whole; binding different parts of a text together to give it a sense of unity

A text can lack cohesion if it jumps suddenly from topic to topic, or if the ideas conflict with one another or aren't in a logical order. Variations in the style of language or in the narrative voice can also make a text hard to understand. The result can be a confused and frustrated reader!

Activity 1.4.1

Have you read a text that didn't make sense? What made it difficult to follow? What do you think the author could have done differently?

How to use connectives

Connectives are words that join different parts of a text. Connectives make connections between parts of a sentence, sentences in a paragraph, and paragraphs in a chapter.

Key term

connective: a word used to connect words, phrases, clauses and sentences

Connectives contribute to the cohesion of a text because they can be used to indicate a text's structure or to show the relationship between ideas in a text.

Connectives that show sequence

Some connectives show how a text is sequenced (see Table 1.9 below); that is, they explain the order of events or information and create a sense of time passing.

Table 1.9: Connectives that show sequence

after	first	once
before	meanwhile	second
finally	next	then

These connectives are important in different text types:

- In procedural texts like recipes, sequencing connectives help readers to understand the order of steps.
- In persuasive texts, they help to indicate the development of an argument.
- In narrative texts, they are used to drive the plot forward.

For example, the text below is the beginning of Edgar Allan Poe's short story 'The Fall of the House of Usher'. In these sentences, connectives convey the passage of time and the narrator's approach to the house.

The Fall of the House of Usher

During the whole of a dull, dark, and soundless day in the autumn of the year, when the clouds hung oppressively low in the heavens, I had been passing alone, on horseback, through a singularly dreary tract of country; and at length found myself, as the shades of the evening drew on, within view of the melancholy House of Usher.

Connectives that link causes and effects

Some connectives join causes with their effects (see Table 1.10 below); that is, they indicate how an action or event (the cause) can create another action or event (the effect). Some examples are listed in the table below.

These connectives are effective in persuasive texts because they suggest something is logical and therefore true.

Table 1.10: Connectives that link causes and effects

accordingly	for this reason	so
as a result of	leading to	such as
because	on account of	therefore
consequently	since	thus

Connectives that compare

Some connectives point out the similarities or differences between things (see Table 1.11 below).

These connectives are effective in persuasive texts because they can be used to show similarities or differences in arguments and points of view.

Table 1.11: Connectives that compare

Similarities	both	like	likewise	similar to	similarly
Differences	conversely	in contrast	on the other hand	unlike	whereas

Structuring your ideas is also discussed in Section 10.2 (page 122).

Activity 1.4.2

1 **Choose a page in a book you are reading and write down all the connectives you can see on that page. Highlight all the sequencing connectives. Underline the connectives that link a cause with an effect. Circle the connectives that compare two things.**

2 **Write three sentences that use connectives from the tables above and on the previous page. Use two different types of connectives in each sentence.**

How to use signals

Many authors use **signals** to show readers how they have organised the information and ideas in their texts. Signals help readers understand a text's structure.

Key term

signal: a word or phrase that lets the reader know about how a text is structured or sequenced

There are different types of signals. These are some of the signals common to informative texts:

- **titles** tell readers what will be discussed in the whole text
- **headings** tell readers what will be discussed in a specific section
- **topic sentences** tell readers what will be discussed in that paragraph (e.g. 'I am about to discuss …') and where the reader is up to in the whole text (e.g. 'In this second argument, I will show you …')
- **introductions** provide an overview or summary of a whole text and outline how the whole text is organised
- **conclusions** or endings tell the reader that the text is ending (e.g. 'In summary, we have seen how …').

In imaginative writing, it is more likely that an author will hint at what is about to happen, rather than signal it explicitly. For example, they might describe dark clouds or stormy weather to signal a dangerous turn of events. This is called **foreshadowing**.

Key term

foreshadowing: a warning or indication of something, often an event, to come

Activity 1.4.3

1. **Reread the extract from 'The Fall of the House of Usher' on page 24. What do you think will happen next? What clues in the text make you think this?**
2. **Look at a page in your science textbook. List the signals you can see.**

An example of structure and sequence

In Table 1.12, a persuasive text from an article in *The Conversation* has been placed in the left-hand column. In this text, Blair Williams argues that the voting age in Australia should be lowered from 18 to 16. In the right-hand column of the table, there are notes explaining the devices Williams has used to signal structure and sequence his ideas.

Table 1.12: The devices used to signal structure and sequence ideas

Sample text	Devices used to signal structure and sequence ideas
Should Australia lower the voting age to 16 like the UK? We asked 5 experts.	• **Signal:** The title of the article tells the reader what is going to be discussed. It also tells the reader that Williams is one of the '5 experts' giving their opinion, indicating that he is knowledgeable about the topic.
I am in full support of reducing the voting age in Australia to 16. Research has shown young people care passionately about political issues, such as addressing the climate crisis, social justice and equality, and mental health.	• **Signal:** The topic sentence states the author's opinion and signals that the rest of the text will present reasons and evidence to support this opinion. • **Connective:** The phrase 'such as' introduces a list of examples.

(continued)

Table 1.12: The devices used to signal structure and sequence ideas (continued)

Sample text	Devices used to signal structure and sequence ideas
However, young Australians are underrepresented in politics, both in terms of representatives as well as issues that affect them. The 2019 Australian Human Rights Commission's report to the United Nations highlighted that young people under the age of 18 feel they do not have a voice. Young Australians should have the right to share their concerns and have a say in their futures at the ballot box.	• **Connective that compares:** The word 'however' signals that a contrasting or conflicting idea is about to be presented: young people 'care passionately', but it is difficult for them to 'have a say'. This also sets up a problem–solution structure. A problem is posed, and then the solution is explained.
There are three key reasons why we should extend the right to vote to 16- and 17-year-olds.	• **Signal**: The phrase 'three key reasons' tells the reader that the reasons are about to be explained by the author.
First, it's an issue of equality. Young Australians aged 16 or 17 are legally able to: engage in paid employment, pay taxes, enlist in the defence forces, marry (with court approval), get a driver's and even a pilot's license, and give medical consent. But they aren't allowed to enjoy a basic right to cast their vote and hold politicians and governments accountable.	• **Connective that shows sequence**: The word 'first' indicates that the three reasons will be numbered, helping the reader to follow the argument. • **Signal**: In this topic sentence, the key word is 'equality', which indicates that this concept will be central to this paragraph. • **Connective that compares:** The word 'but' tells the reader that the author is about to point out differences (i.e. they will list some examples of inequality).
Second, greater youth engagement. International research shows countries that have lowered the voting age to 16 enjoy higher rates of youth political engagement. Expanding the right to vote acknowledges that young people are politically active and encourages them to be more engaged in the formal political arena. If young people feel they have some influence, it might also encourage even greater participation in politics – rather than just aimlessly screaming into the void, or doomscrolling TikTok.	• **Connective that shows sequence:** The word 'second', in addition to the new paragraph, signals that the next reason is being presented. • **Signal:** The phrase 'research shows' introduces supporting evidence or examples. This is a typical argument structure: the author states a reason or opinion, then gives supporting evidence. Common forms of evidence include statistics, case studies and anecdotes.

(continued)

Table 1.12: The devices used to signal structure and sequence ideas (continued)

Sample text	Devices used to signal structure and sequence ideas
Third, this is, ultimately, about creating a more inclusive (and accountable) democracy. Granting the vote to 16- and 17-year-olds will give more young people greater power over issues and concerns that affect them and their peers. And, as there are votes in the mix, politicians would finally have to take note of this overlooked cohort.	• **Connective that shows sequence:** The word 'third' shows the reader that the last reason is about to be explained. • **Signal:** The word 'ultimately' signals that the author is reaching the end of their argument with possibly their strongest reason.

Activity 1.4.4

Find a short media text (e.g. a news article, letter to the editor, opinion piece) and create a table like the one above. Identify and explain the devices that the author has used to achieve cohesion.

CHAPTER 2

Using language to express your ideas

2.1 How to use clauses and sentences to explain ideas

Two of the most important tools in your writing toolbox are **sentences** and **clauses**. To understand how best to use sentences and clauses, you need to understand all their different kinds and how they work.

Key terms

sentence: a group of words that expresses a complete thought; it begins with a capital letter and ends with a full stop, question mark or exclamation mark

clause: a set of words including at least one subject and one verb

Make your writing exciting!

A great way to make your writing more engaging, readable and clear is to use a variety of different kinds of sentences. Overusing one kind of sentence can make a piece of writing feel boring and repetitive.

For example, read the following paragraph.

> I went birdwatching today. My family came with me. I got my binoculars out. I cleaned them. You can't see birds through dirty binoculars. Then we headed off. We took the train. We saw a huge flock of ravens! I had a great time at the park. Lots of ducks were swimming. They were enjoying the sun. What a fun day!

This paragraph uses only one kind of sentence, called a **simple sentence**. This makes the paragraph tiring to read and it isn't very engaging.

The following paragraph is similar to the one above, but some of the simple sentences have been changed.

> I went birdwatching today, and my family came with me. Before we left, I got my binoculars out and cleaned them because you can't see birds through dirty binoculars. Then we headed off. While we were on the train, we saw a huge flock of ravens! I had a great time at the park. Lots of ducks were swimming and enjoying the sun. What a fun day!

The second paragraph is much more engaging and enjoyable to read because it has multiple sentence structures.

Activity 2.1.1

Select a book you're reading this year for school and look at how the sentences are structured. Are they all structured similarly or does the author use a variety of sentence structures?

Introduction to clauses

To understand how sentences work, it's important to understand clauses.

A clause is a group of words that includes a **subject** and a **verb**. Clauses can include other things too, but they need at least one subject and one verb.

Key terms

subject: the person or thing doing an action; the subject is the one 'doing' the verb

verb: a word that describes an action, occurrence or state of being; a 'doing' word

Table 2.1 shows some clauses, and identifies the subject and the verb in each clause.

Table 2.1: Examples of clauses with their subjects and verbs

Clause	Subject	Verb
I eat carrots	I	eat
the dog slept	the dog	slept
you win	you	win
Maria is hilarious	Maria	is
it was gloomy	it	was

Key understanding

If you are trying to figure out which part of a clause is the subject, find the verb (the 'doing' word) and think about who or what is *doing* the verb.

Remember that the subject is usually located *before* the verb.

Activity 2.1.2

In the following clauses, circle the subject and underline the verb.

1 **Ella is happy.**

2 **Tuyen reads a lot of books.**

3 **The pride of lions roared.**

4 **I ate my dinner happily.**

Main clauses and subordinate clauses

There are two types of clauses: **main clause** and **subordinate clause**.

- A main clause is a main piece of information. It can stand on its own as a full sentence. For example, 'I eat broccoli', 'Jaya was tired' and 'the mice ran'.
- A subordinate clause *cannot* stand on its own as a full sentence. It adds extra information or ideas to the main clause. For example, 'while I sleep', 'though she hates eating chocolate' and 'because it is cold' are all subordinate clauses: they need to be attached to a main clause to make sense.

A subordinate clause usually has a **subordinating conjunction** that joins it to the main clause. These include words like 'which', 'because', 'although' and 'after'.

Key terms

main clause: a main piece of information that can stand on its own as a sentence; also called an independent clause

subordinate clause: extra information that cannot stand on its own as a sentence; usually includes a subordinating conjunction; also called a dependent clause

subordinating conjunction: a word that introduces clauses that add information (e.g. 'after', 'when', 'because', 'if', 'that')

Key fact

'Subordinate' means 'less important' – the subordinate clause is less important to the sentence than the main clause. This can help you remember that if a subordinate clause is deleted, the sentence will still make sense without it.

In the following examples, the main clause of each sentence is underlined and the subordinate clause is bolded.

After I ate five pancakes, <u>I went home</u>.

<u>Cara went to the cinema</u> **because she loves movies**.

Unless you leave right now, <u>you will be late</u>.

Table 2.2 lists the steps of writing a main clause and a subordinate clause.

Table 2.2: Steps for writing a main clause and a subordinate clause

Main clause	
Step	**Example**
Write the subject.	The elephants
Choose a verb.	roll
Write the rest of the clause, including any other information after the verb.	The elephants roll in the mud
Subordinate clause	
Step	**Example**
Write a subordinating conjunction.	While
Add the subject.	While you
Choose a verb.	climbed
Write the rest of the clause, including other information after the verb.	While you climbed the mountain
If the subordinate clause comes before a main clause, add a comma at the end.	While you climbed the mountain,

There are many subordinating conjunctions. Table 2.3 shows some common examples.

Table 2.3: Common subordinating conjunctions

after	although	as	as soon as
because	before	even though	if
in case	now that	rather than	since
though	until	when	whenever
where	whether	while	why

Key understanding

Subordinate clauses can be located at the beginning, middle or end of a sentence. This means that they can occur *before* the main clause, *in the middle of* a main clause or *after* a main clause.

For example:

- Even though my dog likes to bark, he is never aggressive. (before)
- My dog, who is never aggressive, likes to bark. (middle)
- My dog likes to bark, although he is never aggressive. (after)

Activity 2.1.3

1 In the following sentences, underline the main clauses and circle the subordinate clauses.

a I am Katherine although everyone calls me Kat.

b My garden, where I grow roses, is blooming.

2 Write a few sentences about your favourite book or movie, using both main clauses and subordinate clauses.

Sentence structures

Now that you understand clauses, you're ready to use them in sentences.

Four different sentence structures are:

- simple sentences
- compound sentences
- complex sentences
- compound-complex sentences.

These different sentence structures all use clauses in different ways.

Simple, compound and complex sentences

Simple and complex sentences

A **simple sentence** is made up of one main clause. For example:

'They like apple pie.'

'Pradeep is sick today.'

On the other hand, a **complex sentence** includes both a main clause and at least one subordinate clause. You can turn a simple sentence into a complex sentence by adding another subordinate clause – a clause that includes a subordinating conjunction (e.g. 'unless', 'after', 'because').

Key terms

simple sentence: a sentence made up of one main clause

complex sentence: a sentence with a main clause and at least one subordinate clause

The following examples are complex sentences, with each subordinate clause underlined.

'They like apple pie because Mum used to bake it.'

'Pradeep is sick today, although he was healthy yesterday.'

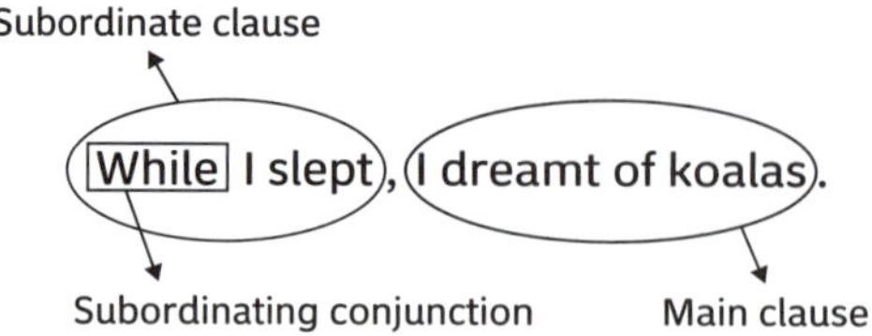

Breaking down a complex sentence

Compound sentences

A **compound sentence** is made up of two or more main clauses joined together. You make a compound sentence by connecting main clauses using a **coordinating conjunction** like 'or', 'and' or 'but'.

Key terms

compound sentence: a sentence made up of at least two main clauses, joined together with a coordinating conjunction

coordinating conjunction: a word that links individual words or groups of words within a sentence (e.g. and, or, but); it joins similar elements equally (e.g. subject + subject or clause + clause)

There are seven coordinating conjunctions in English. You can use the acronym FANBOYS to remember these.

F	A	N	B	O	Y	S
For	And	Nor	But	Or	Yet	So

For example, the following are examples of compound sentences (with the coordinating conjunctions underlined).

Dorothy is a child, and Toto is a dog.

Ngan will drive the car, but I will navigate.

If you imagine that clauses are like bricks, then conjunctions are the mortar that binds the bricks together.

Activity 2.1.4

1 **Write two simple sentences about an experience that made you laugh.**
2 **Combine these simple sentences into a compound sentence using a coordinating conjunction.**
3 **Write a complex sentence about what you are doing next weekend.**

Compound-complex sentences

A **compound-complex sentence** is a mix between a compound sentence and a complex sentence. It has elements of both – like an ice cream with two flavours.

Key term

compound-complex sentence: a sentence that includes at least two main clauses linked with a coordinating conjunction, as well as at least one subordinate clause

A compound-complex sentence has elements of both compound and complex sentences, like an ice cream with two flavours.

A compound-complex sentence has two main clauses connected by a coordinating conjunction (like a compound sentence), as well as at least one subordinate clause (like a complex sentence).

Here is an example of a compound-complex sentence.

Although I play basketball, my brother plays soccer and our sister prefers tennis.

The elements to put together a compound-complex sentence can be seen in Table 2.4.

Table 2.4: Elements of a compound-complex sentence

Elements	Example
Subordinate clause, including a subordinating conjunction	Although I play basketball,
Main clause	my brother plays soccer
Coordinating conjunction	and
Main clause	our sister prefers tennis
Final result	Although I play basketball, my brother plays soccer, and our sister prefers tennis.

Activity 2.1.5

1 **Combine the following simple sentences and conjunctions to make a compound-complex sentence.**

I made dinner　　our parents were away　　because　　I didn't like it　　but

2 **Write a compound-complex sentence about one of your hobbies, using the steps in Table 2.4 as a guide.**

Using complex and compound-complex sentences

Complex and compound-complex sentences can be useful in your writing to show nuanced connections between ideas.

The subordinate clauses in these sentences add additional information. They provide more details that can explain why something is happening; what happened before, after or during an event; the conditions under which something will happen; the difference or similarity between concepts; and many other types of information.

For example, consider how the following complex sentence structure allows the author to compare ideas.

> While the hero is optimistic, the villain thinks the world will never improve.

Compound-complex sentences are often the longest kinds of sentences and can be used to extend, explain and elaborate on ideas. This makes them especially useful in adding complexity and detail to your analytical writing.

For example, consider how the following compound-complex sentence structure allows the author to show cause and effect.

> Because of the hero's optimism, the villain redeems herself and the world is saved.

This is a more nuanced way of writing than simply listing ideas without linking them to each other.

Understanding editing sentences

Using a variety of sentence structures is a great way to level up your writing skills.

When you're editing your work, you can check how well you have incorporated different sentence structures into your writing.

Check if you have lots of simple sentences in a row. Try to combine some into compound or complex sentences to make your writing more advanced.

Make sure that your compound, complex or compound-complex sentences are not so long that they are difficult to read. You could split up some of these, so they are easier to read.

For more information on editing your own work, go to Section 11.2 on page 139.

Activity 2.1.6

Think of an opinion that you hold, such as a social issue you feel strongly about, or a food you like or dislike. Write about this opinion in a few complex and compound-complex sentences, using subordinate clauses to add nuance (e.g. explaining why you hold this opinion or contrasting it with what others think).

Putting sentences into action

Table 2.5 summarises the four different sentence structures discussed in this section, with examples.

Table 2.5: Different sentence structures with examples

Sentence structure	Components	Example
Simple sentence	One main clause	The cat sat on the mat.
Compound sentence	Two or more main clauses	The cat sat on the mat and the dog ate breakfast.
Complex sentence	One main clause with one or more subordinate clauses	While I read a book, the cat sat on the mat.
Compound-complex sentence	Two or more main clauses and one or more subordinate clauses	While I read a book, the cat sat on the mat and the dog ate breakfast.

Remember, just because simple sentences are called 'simple', this doesn't mean you can't use them to write about complicated ideas. Consider this example: 'The square of the hypotenuse of a right-angled triangle equals the sum of the squares of the two other sides.' This is a simple sentence, but it's explaining a complicated mathematical concept.

Similarly, complex and compound-complex sentence structures can be used to express simple ideas. For example:

- 'After I arrived home, I played a game.' (complex)
- 'When we were at the beach, Dad sunbathed and Mum went swimming.' (compound-complex)

Both sentences are easier to understand than the simple sentence about maths.

Activity 2.1.7

Write a paragraph of five or six sentences about something fun you did recently. Make sure you include simple, complex, compound and compound-complex sentences.

2.2 How to use tenses and verbs to communicate clearly

Understanding tenses

The **tense** of a word shows us *when* an action takes place. Using the correct tense in a sentence helps to make the meaning of the sentence clearer.

Key term

tense: a grammatical category that is marked by a verb and used to show when an action takes place

Verbs and simple tense

The tense of a sentence is made clear through the **verbs** used in that sentence.

A verb can be written in the **past**, **present** or **future tense**:

- The past tense shows that something has already happened.
- The present tense shows that something is happening now.
- The future tense shows that something will happen in the future.

Past, present and future tense are the **simple tenses**. See Table 2.6, which shows the simple tenses of three verbs.

Key term

simple tenses: the most basic forms of the past, present and future tenses (e.g. I eat, I ate, I will eat)

Table 2.6: Examples of the simple tenses

Verb	Past tense	Present tense	Future tense
to listen	listened	listen or listens	will listen
to wake	woke	wake or wakes	will wake
to think	thought	think or thinks	will think

Specific text types are often written in certain tenses. For example:

- recipes are written in the present tense (e.g. 'Boil the pasta, then drain it.')
- recounts are written in the past tense (e.g. 'I went to the zoo on the weekend.')

In a piece of writing, it's important that the tense stays consistent. If your writing constantly switches between tenses, the reader may find the text difficult to follow. For example, read the following paragraph.

> Yesterday, I saw a movie with my friends. Before the movie starts, we will buy our popcorn and snacks. The advertisements had gone on for ages! It is a very boring movie, so we have left halfway through it.

This paragraph is very confusing because the tenses are all mixed up! Now read this paragraph.

> Yesterday, I saw a movie with my friends. Before the movie started, we bought our popcorn and snacks. The advertisements went on for ages! It was a very boring movie, so we left halfway through it.

This version stays in the past tense all the way through, and its meaning is much clearer.

Key understanding

You should decide which verb tense your piece of writing will be written in before you start writing. Try to use the same tense for the whole piece. You can write a note to yourself to remind you which tense you have chosen.

Verb groups and tense

Further information about the time when an action takes place can be expressed by adding an **auxiliary verb**.

An auxiliary verb (or 'helping' verb) can go before the main verb of a sentence to provide more information about the tense. Auxiliary verbs include 'have', 'be' and 'will'. An auxiliary verb combined with a main verb is called a **verb group**.

Key terms

auxiliary verb: called a 'helping verb' because it gives more information about the main verb in a sentence, such as by indicating tense

verb group (or verb phrase): a group of words working together in a sentence to express an action or state of being; a verb group typically contains a main verb and auxiliary verbs or adverbs

For example, the following sentences have both auxiliary verbs and main verbs. The auxiliary verbs are underlined and the main verbs are in bold.

- She <u>is</u> **going**.
- We <u>had</u> **won**.
- They <u>have</u> **arrived**.
- You <u>will</u> **eat**.

It is also possible to use multiple auxiliary verbs at the same time; for example, 'Jax has been walking'.

You can express many nuances of time using different tenses and auxiliary verbs. Table 2.7 provides examples of how different tenses can change the meaning of a sentence. Note that auxiliary verbs can have different forms. For example, the auxiliary verb 'have' can also have the form 'had'.

Table 2.7: Examples of sentences with different verb tenses, using the verb 'to walk'

	Past	Present	Future
Simple tense	I **walked** to school last week.	I **walk** to school every day.	I **will walk** to school on Friday.
'Have' auxiliary verb	I **had walked** to school before it started to rain.	I **have walked** to school twice this month.	I **will have walked** to school dozens of times by November.
'Be' auxiliary verb	I **was walking** to school when it started to rain.	I **am walking** to school right now.	I **will be walking** to school every Friday next month.
'Have' + 'be' auxiliary verbs	I **had been walking** to school for years before I injured my leg.	I **have been walking** to school for many years.	I **will have been walking** to school for four years by next February.

Key understanding

Verb tenses can express many different meanings about when an action takes place, as well as other information like whether the action is still happening, has finished or is repeated.

For example, the present tense doesn't always mean *right now*.

It can be used to express something you do regularly (e.g. 'I swim on Tuesdays.') or a timeless truth (e.g. 'Dogs always wag their tails.').

The present tense can also express something happening in the future (e.g. 'We are going to the outdoor cinema on the weekend.').

Activity 2.2.1

1 Convert the following sentences to the tense indicated in brackets.

  a I dance. (past tense)

  b They will skate. (present tense)

  c He was researching sharks. (future tense)

2 Read the following two sentences. Explain what you think is the difference in their meanings.

- I draw with charcoal.
- I am drawing with charcoal.

Verb tense in compound, complex and compound-complex sentences

Keeping the tense consistent within each sentence is part of creating clear pieces of writing. The verb tense should support the meaning you're trying to convey and the timeline of events.

Because compound, complex and compound-complex sentences all have more than one verb, you should make sure that the tense of each verb in the sentence makes sense in combination with the other verbs in the sentence.

For example, Tables 2.8, 2.9 and 2.10 show how verb tenses are used in specific complex, compound and compound-complex sentences.

Table 2.8: Verb tenses in the complex sentence 'I missed my plane because I always run late.'

	Example	Explanation
Main clause	I missed my plane	The writer missed the plane in the past, so past tense is used.
Subordinate clause	because I always run late.	The reason the writer missed the plane is because of a general truth (they always run late), so the present tense is used.

Table 2.9: Verb tenses in the compound sentence 'Weng Yi ate all the chocolate but she will buy some more.'

	Example	Explanation
First main clause	Weng Yi ate all the chocolate	Weng Yi ate all the chocolate in the past, so the past tense is used.
Second main clause	but she will buy some more.	Weng Yi intends to buy more chocolate in the future, so the future tense is used.

Table 2.10: Verb tenses in the compound-complex sentence 'Although I was away for a few days, I had prepared a complete itinerary so Amar knew every detail of the trip.'

	Example	Explanation
Subordinate clause	Although I was away for a few days,	The writer went away in the past, so the past tense is used.
First main clause	I had prepared a complete itinerary	The past tense is used with the auxiliary verb 'have' to show that the itinerary was prepared before the actions in the two other clauses. All the clauses in this sentence are in the past tense, but this clause occurs at the earliest point in time.
Second main clause	so Amar knew every detail of the trip.	Amar knew the trip details in the past, so the past tense is used.

Activity 2.2.2

1 Read the following sentences. Explain why each clause uses its specific verb tense. Explain how the verb tense supports the sentence's overall meaning.

For example, in the sentence 'While I walked the dog, John cleaned the house', the first clause is in the past tense because it took place in the past, and the second clause is also in the past tense because it takes place at the same time as the first clause.

a I love roller-skating but I will not be at the rink for a long time.

b Because Anastasia had graduated, she took a holiday.

2 Write a paragraph, imagining you are writing an email to a friend. Use some compound, complex and compound-complex sentences. Ensure the tense is consistent across the whole paragraph and within each sentence.

2.3 How images and sound can be used to create perspective

Using images to create perspective

Communication doesn't just occur through written language. Think about the images in graphic novels, picture books and animated cartoons. All of these images communicate with their **audience**.

Key term

audience: an intended or assumed group of readers, listeners or viewers that a writer, designer, filmmaker or speaker is addressing

Note that there are two types of images:

- **still images** (static, fixed, unmoving) – e.g. photographs, paintings, illustrations and advertisements such as billboards
- **moving images** – e.g. animated cartoons and advertisements such as commercials.

Creators of visual texts manipulate the elements of images to convey ideas and meaning, and to influence how viewers interpret images. Features of images that affect a viewer's perspective include the:

- **content** of an image
- **composition** of the image.

Analysing the content of images

Use the questions in Table 2.11 below to develop your understanding of how the content of an image contributes to its meaning and influences how a viewer understands it.

Table 2.11: Elements that make up the **content** of an image

Element	Questions to consider
Subject	• Who or what is the focus of the image? • Why do you think the creator has chosen this subject? (e.g. What message is the creator sending? What issue or theme are they exploring?)
Setting	• What are the time and place shown in the image? • Why do you think the creator has chosen this setting? (e.g. What does the setting tell us about the subject?)
Background	• What details are shown in the background of the image? • What do these background details tell the viewer? (e.g. Do they provide information about the subject?)
Colour	• What are the main colours in the image? • Are these colours associated with particular qualities or ideas? (e.g. Green is often associated with envy and red with anger.) • Do these colours evoke any feelings in the viewer?
Symbols	• Can you see any symbols in the image? (Symbols are objects that represent ideas or feelings; e.g. a dove can represent peace.)

Activity 2.3.1

The image below is an illustration from a graphic novel. Carefully look at the image, then fill in the following table to analyse the image. Use Table 2.11 to help you.

Element	Analysis
Subject	
Setting	
Background	
Colour	
Symbols	

Analysing the composition of images

It is not just through the content of an image that creators can communicate with their audience. The composition of an image can also convey ideas and meaning and can influence how viewers interpret images.

Two key elements of the composition of photographic images are camera angles and shot sizes:

- The **camera angle** is the angle at which the camera is pointed at the subject.
- **Shot size** refers to how much of a subject is included in an image.

Table 2.12 below describes the different camera angles and shot sizes and explains how these can convey meaning.

Table 2.12: Camera angles and shot sizes

Camera angle	Example	Shot size	Example
A **high camera angle** shows characters and objects from above. It might make you feel more powerful than the character.		An **extreme long shot** is used to set a scene and give you an overview of a particular location or setting.	
A **low camera angle** shows characters and objects from below. It usually shows the importance or power of characters.		A **long shot** often introduces characters in a scene or provides more information about a setting.	
An **eye-level camera angle** shows a character or an object at the same level as you. It is often used to express fairness or equality with the subject.		A **medium shot** is often used to show what a character is doing or to capture them speaking.	
A **bird's-eye camera angle** captures a scene or object by looking directly down from far above it, like how a flying bird would see things.		A **close-up shot** is often used to draw attention to facial expressions or objects.	
A **point-of-view camera angle** captures a scene from the perspective of a character.		An **extreme close-up** is often used to draw attention to very small details on objects or people.	

Some other elements that contribute to the composition of images are explained in Table 2.13.

Table 2.13: Other elements that make up the **composition** of an image

Element	Explanation
Framing	The way in which elements are included within the frame (the outside boundary of an image) or excluded from it. Strong framing creates a sense of enclosure around elements, while weak framing creates a sense of openness.
Proximity	This refers to the distances between the different elements in an image and what this may mean. (e.g. Why are two figures close to each other? Does this mean they're friends or allies?)
Salience	A strategy of highlighting what is important in a text (e.g. a person, object or idea). In images, salience is created by placing an item in the foreground, manipulating size or using contrast in tone or colour.
Social distance	This refers to the distance between people in the image: are they close or far apart? What does tell the viewer?
Sizing	This refers to the different sizes of the elements, how these sizes relate to each other and what they mean. (e.g. Why is one person larger than another person?)
Vectors	Visual lines that aid direction and movement; also called leading lines because they lead the viewer's eyes to a particular point in an image.

Activity 2.3.2

Look at the image from a graphic novel on page 44.

1 a What 'camera' angle has been used for this image?

b Why do you think the creator used this camera angle?

2 a What shot size has been used for this image?

b Why do you think the creator used this shot size?

3 Why do you think the central figure is positioned so close to the car? What might this tell us about the relationship between these two elements?

4 What elements of the image do you think are important? How can you tell? (Hint: Look at 'salience' in Table 2.13.)

Animated cartoons

An animated cartoon is a form of visual communication that usually tells a story. Animation is the process of bringing illustrations to life by making it seem as though they are moving. Animated cartoons can be created by hand drawing a series of illustrations, by using stop motion (a technique where the camera is stopped and started between frames to record tiny movements or by using computer software to bring static images to life (a process called computer-generated animation or CGA).

Animated cartoons can be created by drawing a series of illustrations that when viewed in quick succession create a sense of movement.

Think about it

What kind of animations do you watch? Why do you like to watch them? What stories do they tell and how do they do this?

Animations exist outside of movies and TV shows – keep an eye out for them in your everyday life and have a think about what their purpose is and what they are trying to communicate.

Activity 2.3.3

One of the first animated cartoons featured Mickey Mouse. It is called 'Steamboat Willie' and was released in 1928. Watch this cartoon (you can find it on YouTube) and then answer the following questions.

1. **What is the setting of this animated cartoon? How can you tell?**
2. **Describe the personality of Mickey. How did you work this out?**
3. **a What is the main camera angle used in this animated cartoon?**

   b Why do you think the creator mainly used this camera angle?
4. **a What shots were used in the animation?**

   b Why do you think the creator used these shots?

Using images and sound to create perspective

Some creators communicate with the audience of their texts – and influence the audience's perspective on the text – by using multiple modes. These texts are called **multimodal texts**.

Key term

multimodal texts: texts that combine two or more communication modes, which may include the written mode (written words), the visual mode (still and moving images) and the auditory mode (spoken words, music and other sounds); multimodal texts include advertisements, television programs and films

Analysing sound in texts

'Sound' in a text includes spoken words, music and sound effects. Sounds can be used to evoke emotions, create a mood, guide the viewers' attention, provide information about settings, characters and events, and enhance the meaning conveyed by a text.

Use the questions in Table 2.14 to develop your understanding of how sound in a text contributes to the overall impact and meaning, and how sound can influence a viewer's response to still or moving images.

Table 2.14: Sound in texts

Sound	Examples	Questions to consider
Spoken words	A voice-over Characters speaking	• What information do the spoken words convey? • In what tone are the words spoken?
Music	A well-known song A jingle	• Does the music create a particular mood? What effect does this have on the viewer? • Does the music suggest a particular attitude to the subject of an image? • Does the music create context for a person? (e.g. Does it establish a historical period, or reinforce aspects of a character, such as class and culture?)
Sound effects	Footsteps, animal noises, environmental sounds like rain	• What are the purpose and impact of the sound effects? (e.g. Do they make the text funny? Or make the text seem more real?)

Key term

jingle: a short, catchy song or tune, typically used in advertising, that is designed to be memorable and promote a product or brand

Advertisements

An advertisement is a multimodal text that publicly promotes a product or service. The primary purpose of an advertisement is to persuade a target audience to buy a product or service, or to change a behaviour.

Many advertisements are excellent examples of texts that combine images and sound. Here are some historical Australian advertisements that you can look up:

- example of spoken words: the Solo man ad (1986)
- example of music: the jingle in the 'I like Aeroplane Jelly' advertisement (1930s)
- example of sound effects: the 'Sounds of a KitKat bar' television advertisement (2015).

Activity 2.3.4

Look up one of the famous Australian advertisements listed above or find your own advertisement that uses sound. Analyse the use of sound in that advertisement, using Table 2.14 to help you.

2.4 How to use specialist vocabulary

You may have noticed that you use different words for different subjects. For example, you use words like 'algebra' and 'pi' in maths, and 'narrative' and 'perspective' in English. Understanding the meanings of the specialist words used in a subject will build your knowledge of that subject and will also assist you to clearly communicate your ideas.

Think about it

What are some words you use in subjects like music or science? Did you have to look up these words when you first heard them?

Sometimes, words have an everyday meaning and a specialist meaning. Can you think of any words like this?

The first step in using specialist vocabulary is to make sure you understand the exact, correct meaning of the words you are using. When you come across a word you don't know, use the following steps to understand it.

- **Look at the context clues:** How has the word been used? What do the surrounding words tell you about its meaning? Paying attention to how a word is used in a sentence will help you to understand it.
- **Find the word's definition:** Look up the word in a dictionary or ask your teacher to explain the meaning of the word to you.
- **Practise using the word:** Start using the word when you are writing and speaking. You want to get to the point where you are comfortable using specialist words, and you are using them correctly and naturally.

Key term

context clues: the words and information surrounding an unfamiliar word, which a reader or listener uses to understand its meaning

Activity 2.4.1

1 **Find three unfamiliar words related to a subject at school. Look up the definitions of these words. Use the words in a sentence or two.**

2 **Working with a friend or in a small group, compare the words you selected in Question 1. Then, try using the words in conversation.**

Using academic vocabulary to analyse texts

Academic vocabulary means the specialist words that represent ideas and concepts in a particular subject. Some examples of academic vocabulary for studying English are listed in Table 2.15 below.

Table 2.15: Examples of academic vocabulary

Academic term	Academic meaning
Critique	an analysis, review or assessment of a text
Factor	an element of a text that contributes to the text's purpose; factors in texts include plot, structure, language, genre, characters and themes
Hypothesis	a proposed explanation for an element of a text; an educated guess that is based on textual evidence
Issue	an important topic or subject of discussion or debate

Understanding the meanings of academic terms will improve your knowledge of key concepts in English. Using academic terms will help you to clearly communicate your ideas. Let's look at how the academic vocabulary in Table 2.15 relates to your work in English:

- **Critiquing** a text involves more than just criticising it or deciding whether or not you like it. You need to analyse the text and consider whether the author has succeeded in what they set out to do.
- Which **factors** contribute to the text achieving its purpose? Do any factors get in the way of the author achieving their goal?
- Before you finish reading a text, can you guess (**hypothesise**) what might happen next? These guesses need to be based on textual evidence.

- What **issues** are mentioned in the text? Is the author trying to present a particular point of view on a topic? Identifying the issues in a text shows you have deeply considered and understood that text.

Think about it

Consider a piece of writing you have read recently (e.g. a novel, an article, an essay, a poem). How would you go about critiquing it? Do you have the language to do so? Or are there academic terms you need to learn?

Using specialist vocabulary to write about poetry

In your studies, you will find that understanding and being able to use specialist vocabulary will help you to analyse particular topics and text types, such as poetry. Poetry has distinct elements and conventions, and uses specific techniques (called 'poetic devices'). The names and descriptions of some poetic devices are listed in Table 2.16 below. Understanding the meanings of the specialist terms in Table 2.16 will help you to understand what you notice when reading poetry; it will also assist you to clearly express your ideas about poems.

Table 2.16: Poetic devices

Name of poetic device	Description of poetic device
Alliteration	A recurrence of the same consonant sound at the beginning of words in close succession (e.g. 'ripe, red raspberry')
Assonance	The repetition of a vowel sound in words close together (e.g. rain, main)
Imagery	Descriptive language used to represent objects, actions and ideas in ways that appeal to the senses of a reader or viewer
Metaphor	A comparison where one thing is described as if it *is* another thing
Onomatopoeia	A word or phrase that mimics the sound it describes (e.g. crash, bang)
Personification	A metaphor that gives human qualities to something non-living or inanimate
Rhyme	Matching vowel and consonant sounds at the ends of words
Rhythm	A feeling of movement or pulse produced by a pattern of stressed and unstressed syllables
Simile	A comparison where one thing is described as being similar to something else, using the words 'like' or 'as'
Symbol	An object that represents something else, often an abstract idea or concept

Table 2.17 below shows how we can use specialist terms to identify and analyse the techniques used by a poet. The left-hand column of the table has the first two stanzas of Henry Lawson's poem 'Second class wait here'. The right-hand column identifies the poetic devices Lawson has used and analyses the effects of these devices.

Table 2.17: Example analysis of part of Henry Lawson's 1899 poem 'Second class wait here'

<table>
<tr><th>Lines from the poem</th><th>Analysis of poetic devices</th></tr>
<tr><td>At suburban railway stations – you may see them as you pass –</td><td rowspan="2">The rhyme in the first two lines of the poem builds a sense of rhythm and movement that is akin to a moving train.</td></tr>
<tr><td>there are signboards on the platform saying 'Wait here second class;'</td></tr>
<tr><td>And to me the whirr and thunder and the cluck of running-gear</td><td>Lawson uses onomatopoeia to vividly portray the setting of this poem.</td></tr>
<tr><td>Seem to be forever saying 'Second class wait here –</td><td rowspan="4">Using the same four words in different order creates a rhythm, which contributes to the sense of movement in the poem: like a train chugging along.</td></tr>
<tr><td>Wait here second class</td></tr>
<tr><td>Second class wait here.'</td></tr>
<tr><td>Seem to be forever saying, 'Second class wait here.'</td></tr>
<tr><td>Yes, the second class were waiting in the days of serf and prince,
And the second class are waiting – they've been waiting ever since,</td><td>A serf and a prince are symbols of a bygone era (a serf was a working-class person in the Middle Ages); using these terms indicates that second-class passengers have been waiting a very long time.</td></tr>
<tr><td>There are gardens in the background, and the line is bare and drear,</td><td>This imagery helps readers envision the area around the station, giving the setting of the poem more depth.</td></tr>
<tr><td>Yet they wait beneath a signboard, sneering 'Second class wait here.'</td><td>The use of 'sneering' creates personification as it sounds like the signboard is looking down on the passengers with second-class tickets.</td></tr>
</table>

Activity 2.4.2

Read the poem 'Face of the City' by Grace Perry, which was published around 1960. It is available at: https://ozpoemaday.wordpress.com/2012/02/23/face-of-the-city-by-grace-perry/

1 **Use a dictionary to look up any words you don't understand.**

2 **Identify examples of alliteration, metaphor and personification.**

3 Write a paragraph analysing the poem using specialist language. You can examine how the poem made you feel, how the writer has created imagery or what you think the writer is trying to communicate.

2.5 How to use colons and brackets

You can improve your writing by knowing when to use colons and brackets to make what you are saying clearer.

How to use colons in your writing

Colons (:) draw attention to the information that follows them. They can introduce a subtitle, a list or an example, or extend or clarify the text that appears before the colon. Table 2.18 shows an example of each of these.

Table 2.18: Using colons

Option	Example
A subtitle	Australia's outback: Amazing facts about Australia's interior
A list	Australia's interior has many deserts you can visit, including: the Great Victoria Desert, the Tanami Desert, the Strzelecki Desert and the Great Sandy Desert.
An example	Tourists visiting deserts should remember one thing: always be prepared.
Extending or clarifying text appearing before	Deserts are harsh terrains: care must be taken when exploring them.

Activity 2.5.1

1 Place a colon in each of the following sentences if and where appropriate.

a Exploring the red desert, Phoebe could only think of one word amazing!

b The Australian outback is full of life kangaroos, emus, eucalyptus trees, wattle trees and reptiles.

c Travellers should take plenty of water with them when hitting the road.

2 a Write a sentence that uses a colon to introduce a list.

b Write a sentence that uses a colon to clarify or extend text.

c Write a sentence that uses a colon to introduce an example.

How to use brackets in your writing

Brackets (also called parentheses) are punctuation marks that can be used to:

- add extra information to a sentence
- make what you are saying clearer.

The sentence should still make sense if you take out the information in the brackets. For example:

- UNESCO (the United Nations Educational, Scientific and Cultural Organization) recognises many of Australia's reefs as World Heritage Areas.
- As the climate keeps changing, more Australian reefs are in danger of bleaching events (when stressed corals expel the algae that gives them colour) resulting from rising sea temperatures.
- Cynthia Wong (a professor of sustainable tourism at La Trobe University) has called on the state government to consider technical solutions to help manage visitor numbers.

Activity 2.5.2

1 Put brackets in an appropriate place in the following sentences.

a The Department of Climate Change, Energy, the Environment and Water DCCEEW is responsible for Australia's water policy and resources.

b Bridget Jane owner of Jane Tourism Boats thinks more needs to be done to protect Australia's reefs.

2 Write three sentences that all use brackets.

PART 2 LITERATURE

Literature and contexts

3.1 Exploring ideas in literature from different contexts

As we discussed in Part 1, studying **literature** means looking at different kinds of writing and analysing how these texts work. What ideas are the authors exploring? How has the creator used the characters, events and issues of the story to explore themes?

The **context** of a text is also important. Context refers to the influence that history, culture and society have on an author that is visible in the text. The historical context of a story refers to the time period it was written in and the events in the author's life that may have influenced them. The cultural context refers to the influence of the author's culture on their writing. We can also look at the social context, and ask if there were issues in society at the time that could have affected the author when they were writing. These three contexts are often closely linked.

Key terms

literature: creative works, particularly written works, that are thought to be of high artistic value

context: an environment or situation in which a text is created or responded to

Traditionally, the study of literature in English was mainly focused on the culture of one country: England. And while writers such as Shakespeare and Jane Austen are still important, increasingly we are being encouraged to learn about literature from around the world. This broadens how we look at things and challenges what we assume about the world.

Traditional literature includes Shakespeare's flawed protagonist, Macbeth.

As we live in Australia, it makes sense to read literature written by people who live here. Historically, many Australian writers with European heritage compared Australia to the country they knew. But as we read more

First Nations literature, we begin to understand a broader concept of **Country**, enriching our understanding of what it means to live in Australia. Also, people who have moved to Australia in recent times can bring fresh ideas about what it is like to experience our culture as an outsider.

Key term

Country: (as opposed to 'country') describes the lands and waters to which First Nations peoples are connected; the term contains complex ideas about law, place, custom, language, spiritual belief, cultural practice, material sustenance, family and identity

Exploring literature involves looking at how similar ideas can be looked at from different contexts. This chapter looks at three examples: what it means to be a hero, the pioneering woman's experience told through colonial and First Nations perspectives, and how country and city life are represented by writers from different eras.

Understanding different contexts: literature and the hero

It's in our nature to cheer for the main character when we read a story, which is why so many books follow **the hero's journey**. If you look up the definition of a 'hero', you're likely to find something like 'a person admired for their bravery, achievements and noble qualities'.

Key term

the hero's journey: a common story framework where a hero goes on an adventure, has to overcome a problem or conflict, and returns home a changed person

But not all heroes in literature are the same, which is why we can't define what a hero is too narrowly. Table 3.1 provides examples of different kinds of heroes.

Table 3.1: Heroes in fiction, with examples

Type	Explanation	Examples
The classic hero	A brave person who steps into the heroic role willingly	King Arthur, Harry Potter
The epic hero	A larger-than-life character who completes huge challenges	Hercules, Thor
The reluctant hero	Someone called on to do something brave or noble even though they don't feel up to the task	Frodo Baggins, Katniss Everdeen
The tragic hero	Someone with a fatal flaw in their personality that they can't correct, usually leading to their downfall	Severus Snape, Macbeth
The anti-hero	A flawed, often selfish character who is still a figure of admiration	Han Solo, Harley Quinn

There are many more kinds of heroes – often the kind of hero is shaped by the context of the story. Different historical and social contexts also affect our perception of what is heroic. For example, the epic hero comes from the oral storytelling of ancient Greece, where values of strength and bravery were prized, but where people also felt they had to contend with the whims of gods who could decide their fate.

Meanwhile, in the Australian folksong 'Waltzing Matilda', the hero is a man who steals a sheep, then jumps into a river to escape being caught and drowns! The context for the song was Australia's history as a convict settlement, so anti-heroes who defied authority were admired.

Activity 3.1.1

1 **Reflect on what heroism means to you. Do you have a hero in your life? Who is your favourite fictional hero?**

2 **Research a hero from a culture other than your own. Write three sentences on what makes them heroic. How does the context of their culture change what is viewed as heroic?**

Understanding different contexts: literature from book to film

When adapting a novel or short story to a film or television show, filmmakers often find themselves facing the challenge of balancing the expectations of people who loved the original text with the limitations of what can be shown on screen. Filmmakers often play with the context of the text as well, bringing their own perspectives and experiences to telling a story.

The film *The Drover's Wife: the Legend of Molly Johnson* was written and directed by and starred Goa–Gunggari–Wakka Wakka Murri woman Leah Purcell. It shows how viewing a traditional Australian story through a First Nations lens provides new ideas for exploration.

The story in writing

The original short story, 'The Drover's Wife', was written in 1892 by the Australian writer Henry Lawson. The story follows 24 hours in the life of a woman looking after her four children in outback Australia while her husband is away droving (moving cattle or sheep long distances). She sees a dangerous snake slither under her house, so she stays up all night to protect her family from being bitten.

During the night, she reflects on the other challenges she has endured alone: fire, flood, almost dying in childbirth and being threatened by strangers. Just before dawn, the snake appears, and she and her dog kill it. She has once again survived.

The story explores themes of isolation and resilience but is very much 'of its time'. The country where the woman lives is seen as hostile and unforgiving. The First Nations characters are talked about negatively and looked down on.

The following extract gives you a sense of the story.

> Near midnight. The children are all asleep and she sits there still, sewing and reading by turns. From time to time she glances round the floor and wall-plate, and, whenever she hears a noise, she reaches for the stick. The thunderstorm comes on, and the wind, rushing through the cracks in the slab wall, threatens to blow out her candle ... Alligator [her dog] lies at full length on the floor, with his eyes turned towards the partition. She knows by this that the snake is there. There are large cracks in that wall opening under the floor of the dwelling-house.

Henry Lawson lived from 1867 to 1922. He spent time travelling between the bush and the city, and while he admired the resilience of people who lived in the country, he disliked the romantic descriptions of life in the bush that were popular at the time. He advocated for rights for poor people following the example of his mother, Louisa Lawson, who also campaigned for the rights of women. Lawson's admiration for the toughness of Australian women comes through in the story. However, he did not extend the same admiration to his descriptions of First Nations peoples, instead adopting the racist attitudes of his peers. All these factors are part of the context of the story.

The story on film

In the film, the drover's wife now has a name, Molly Johnson, and more complex relationships with her husband and the other people who live in the area. The film has broadened the scope of the story. It looks not just at a woman protecting her family, but at the conflicts between the First Nations peoples and European colonisers, and what that means in terms of surviving on the land.

Molly struggles not just to survive, but also to be proud of her mixed-race identity in a world that doesn't always accept her. The 'stray blackfellow' of the original story is a far more important character, Yadaka, and his experiences are treated with greater depth. Also, the Australian landscape is shown to be beautiful in the film, rather than only being portrayed as hostile.

This extract from an article about the film provides more context.

> ***The Drover's Wife: the Legend of Molly Johnson* brings a Black woman's perspective to Australian frontier films**
>
> by Megan Carrigy, Associate Director,
> Academic Programs, New York University
>
> ... Citing three generations of drovers in her own family, Purcell explained in a recent interview how, as a five-year-old girl, she would implore her mother to read Lawson's story to her. For Purcell, it was 'the first time I used my imagination and saw myself in a story'. ...

Purcell has been repeatedly drawn to The Drover's Wife as a way of placing her Indigenous family's story before a broad Australian audience. … Purcell gives voice to Indigenous experiences of the frontier that were maligned and marginalised in Lawson's version. …

Yadaka is inspired by Purcell's great-grandfather, Tippo Charlie Chambers, a caring and gentle man who spent time as a travelling circus performer in the 1890s while yearning for his Country. …

The strong bond the drover's wife has with her children in Lawson's original story is deepened in Purcell's film. Molly is driven to protect her children from the authorities and to overcome violence and hardship. …

The way that Purcell's Molly Johnson endures in this film is both inspiring and heartbreaking. This is a subversive survival story that brings an unflinching new perspective to Australian cinema's ongoing engagement with the frontier.

The Conversation, 10 November 2021

The film was released in 2021, 129 years after Henry Lawson wrote the original story.

However, some of the most important themes remain the same across the two versions:

- the resilience required of a young woman alone in the bush, protecting her children
- the vulnerability of being a lone woman when some men can use their greater physical strength to intimidate
- the strength required to work with the country rather than against it.

Taking characters from the page to film is also discussed in Section 4.2 on pages 69–70.

Activity 3.1.2

1 ***The Drover's Wife*** **film is set in 1893, when state governments were enacting laws to 'protect' First Nations peoples, often by taking children away from their parents. How do you think this context might inform the bond of the mother and her children in the film?**

2 **One of the contexts of First Nations literature is that it is based on an oral tradition; that is, stories are spoken and passed down through generations orally rather than being written down. Do you know any First Nations stories, such as those about the Rainbow Serpent or Tiddalik the frog? Did you read these stories or were they told to you? How do you think this context might change your relationship with the story?**

Think about it

Earlier in this chapter, we looked at the context of the hero. Is the drover's wife a hero in Henry Lawson's story? Is she a hero in the film? What actions might make her heroic?

Understanding different contexts: the city and the bush in Australian writing

'The Drover's Wife' provides a stark depiction of bush life, because it was written in an era when Australia had a much smaller and more scattered population and European colonisers were focused on 'taming' the land.

Australia is now a country of more than 27 million people, with 87 per cent of us living along the coast. What does it mean to grow up in the city or the country? How have these things changed over the past few hundred years? Are there any issues that have stayed the same?

Read the extract of the poem below by Ruari Jack Hughes. What does it seem to say about city life?

The City and the City

* with acknowledgments to *The City and The City* by China Miéville

there is the city and there is the city, two territories coinciding
with areas cross-hatched, others overlapping, available
to only one agent — apparently not viable, or so it seems

slide through here and be sure not to notice a thing;
eyes are looking, looking, not seeing, not recognising
that person over there — he's also looking slantwise, avoiding

you and the string of individuals stretching along this side
of the street, though it appears there is no way to step along
without knocking into someone — but you see, I just did

not collide with any of the crowd which seems impenetrable,
so chocker-block squared off with not a split or cross-crack
anywhere, meaning that no space exists for me — and yet,

and yet, I must proceed, can't stay still, can't go backwards;
there is a crime to solve — or a crime to commit, doesn't matter,
just don't stop because stillness will disappear you, nothing left

This poem was written in 2024, in Perth. Does this context provide more insight into what the poet is trying to say? The themes of feeling crowded and invisible are common when discussing city life.

Think about it

Sometimes you will read a poem and not know its context. Do you think context helps readers understand poetry better? Would you rather look at a poem without knowing about the writer? Or do you think it is better to know what the writer intended?

Ruari Jack Hughes has lived in many parts of Australia. He says, 'although I have lived about two-thirds of my life in Western Australia, I didn't intend to settle here and have always felt a bit marooned in the place (perhaps an odd observation) so the sense of dislocation in the poem derives in part from that condition.'

Does knowing this context affect how you feel about the poem?

Activity 3.1.3

1 **There is a piece of context supplied with the poem above – the acknowledgment of the book *The City and The City*. This book involves a murder investigation taking place in two cities that exist side by side but where the people who live in each city are forbidden from visiting or even acknowledging one another. How does this context add meaning to the poem? Pick out three lines in the poem that refer to people not acknowledging one another.**

2 **Activity 2.4.2 on page 52 asked you to read the poem 'Face of the City' by Grace Perry. This poem was written in 1963 while the author was living in Sydney. The early 1960s in Sydney were marked by building projects that transformed the city's skyline. Write a short paragraph explaining how the context of early 1960s Sydney might have influenced how Perry wrote about the city.**

Engaging with literature

4.1 Developing opinions about what you read

When studying English, your opinion is your **subjective** and personal response to a text. We each respond differently to **literary texts**, forming our own opinions about characters, settings and events. Developing opinions helps us to reflect on our experiences and question ideas, feelings and values. Forming opinions about a text also means we are engaging with the literature and connecting with the author's ideas.

Key terms

subjective: a point of view based on personal feelings and opinions rather than on facts

literary texts: past and contemporary texts from a range of cultural contexts that are valued for their form and style and are recognised as having artistic value (e.g. novels, poems, short stories, literary nonfiction)

Many factors shape the opinions we develop in response to a text. Some of these factors are elements of the text itself. Table 4.1 shows some examples.

Table 4.1: Factors that can shape opinions about texts

Factor	Examples
Settings	Familiar or unfamiliar landscapes, realistic or fantastical, indoor and human built or natural wilderness
Themes, ideas and values	Broad themes, such as 'family dynamics' or 'coming of age', or more specific ideas, such as 'holding a grudge only harms ourselves'
Events	Epic and grand (involving whole societies) or intimate and domestic (involving only one or two people)
Choices and consequences	Not only the choices the characters make but also the consequences they experience as a result
Tone	The mood created and the emotions around it
Structure	The order of events and the shape of the story

(continued)

Table 4.1: Factors that can shape opinions about texts (continued)

Factor	Examples
Style	The way in which the story is told, such as fast paced or slow, with rich sensory imagery or with minimal description
Specific language choices	The use of literary devices such as metaphor and simile

The other factor that influences the opinions you form as a reader is your own context. Your context is the world around you and your personal, social and cultural experiences, and your values. Some of the elements of a reader's context are listed in the diagram below.

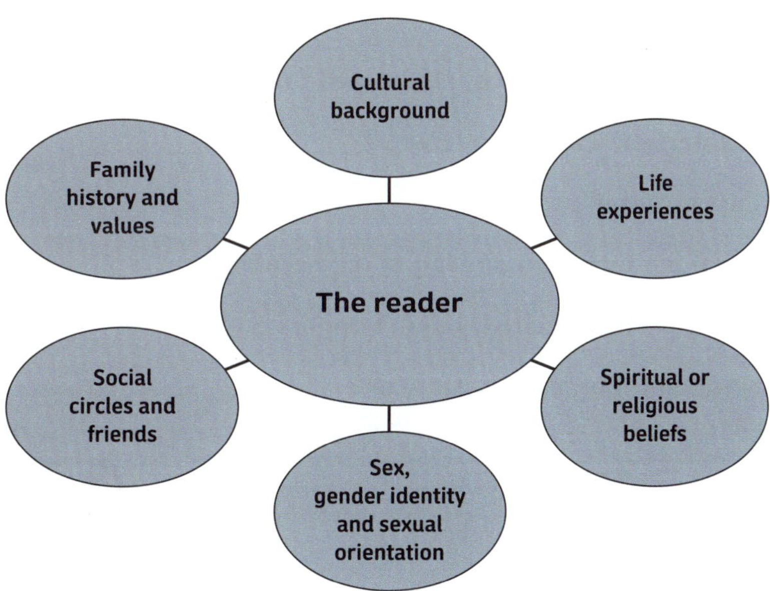

A reader's context consists of many different factors.

Your context may be similar to that of your friends, family members or other readers of the same social setting. But your particular mix of experiences and values is unique to you, so your responses to texts can also be unique.

Activity 4.1.1

1 a Write down two topics you have opinions about; for example, the value of school uniforms or whether people should eat meat.

b Summarise your opinion about each topic in a sentence.

2 Think about the two opinions you expressed in Question 1. What factors shaped these opinions? Which aspects of your context influenced you to form these ideas?

Think about it

Assumptions can influence our opinions, particularly assumptions we aren't aware of. Have you ever made an assumption about someone that turned out to be wrong? Were you surprised?

How to develop an opinion about a text

We're all naturally good at forming quick views about what we like and dislike, but developing opinions about characters, events and texts is a little harder.

One useful way to start developing your opinion about a text is to ask yourself some of the following questions:

- How did the text make me feel?
- Which characters did I feel most connected to, and why?
- Which characters did I dislike, and why?
- Which events took me by surprise?
- Which parts of the text were moving or memorable?
- Were there any parts of the text I didn't understand?
- Did the characters' journeys frustrate or satisfy me?
- If I had written this text, would I have changed anything about the ending? If so, why?

In response to these questions, you can start to form statements that summarise your opinions; for example, 'I didn't like the main character's best friend, because his actions seemed selfish' or 'The text shows that we can't always predict the outcomes of our actions'.

Uncover *why* you like a text by asking yourself questions that develop your opinion.

Activity 4.1.2

Choose a short text, such as a short story, video, blog post or podcast episode. Write one or two paragraphs stating your opinion about the text. What do you think is its central message? What were its strengths or weaknesses? What did it make you think about?

How to justify your opinion about a text

When you are discussing and comparing your opinions about texts with others, being able to back up or justify your ideas can help people understand your point of view. This means you need to be able to show which parts of the text shaped your response. This may include things that characters or the narrator have said, or behaviours, values, actions, consequences and events represented in the text.

You can also justify your opinion by using what you can **infer** from a text. Inferences are assumptions or guesses we make about a text. Often, writers suggest ideas in texts but don't explicitly state these ideas. Readers pick up on these ideas by piecing together clues in the text (e.g. characters' actions, what they say) and drawing conclusions from these hints.

Key term

infer: figure out what a writer is suggesting in the text, but not necessarily stating obviously

Often an opinion on a text (or on particular characters or events) could form the basis for a class discussion or a written response. This is sometimes described as a contention or **main contention**. You may be asked to provide **textual evidence** to back up your opinion.

Key terms

main contention: the central argument of your essay, or the summary of your response to the essay question or topic; you should be able to express a contention in one simple sentence

textual evidence: examples from your text that support your interpretation; often these are quotations, but they can also be other parts of the text such as events, settings, characters and relationships

Choose, collect and record evidence and use it to support your opinions and responses to the text.

You can collect evidence from your text in many ways. Some people find it best not to interrupt their first reading of a text by taking any notes, but others find they need to underline or take notes the first time they see a text so they don't forget important ideas. Either way, when you begin to record textual evidence, you should *always* record the page number with the quote or information.

Ways to collect textual evidence include:

- making notes in the margins (if you own a physical copy of the text)
- using sticky notes to mark pages and write notes (especially if you have a library copy!) or writing notes in a notebook
- saving notes on a device
- using voice notes on your phone (although this can be harder to access later; you might want to listen back and transcribe relevant notes).

Whichever way you do it, you'll need a way of sorting your evidence into groups so you can easily find the pieces you need later. Different strategies will suit different people and texts. Experiment and find the one that works best for you. Some possible ways to categorise textual evidence are to sort your quotes according to:

A detective needs evidence to prove who committed a crime; you need evidence to justify your opinions.

- character
- section of text (such as chapters)
- theme or key idea
- kind of evidence (e.g. character quotes, events, descriptions, language features).

Depending on your methods, you might also find coloured pens, highlighting, tables, graphic organisers or sticky labels helpful.

Understand: choosing and using evidence

- Be accurate in what you quote: use the exact punctuation, words and spelling the writer has used, otherwise you may not be justifying your opinion reliably.
- Choose short quotes (usually a maximum of around 30 words) so that when you discuss them, you can focus on your own ideas about the text.
- Be aware of the context of what you are quoting: where is it in the text, and what other important events or plot elements might be connected?
- Choose evidence from a range of sources in the text (i.e. quote dialogue from multiple characters; use evidence from throughout the text, not just the first few pages).
- Understand the meaning of any evidence you use – not just the individual words, but how the evidence relates to the rest of the text.
- Use quotes or evidence that are self-contained (i.e. do not need lots of explanation to contextualise); also make sure the grammar is still clear out of the original context.
- Make sure your quotes are relevant and convincing.

When you justify an opinion, you need to explain how and why parts of the text back up what you're thinking. For example, you might have the opinion that 'The text shows that nobody is completely moral all the time.' You might support this opinion by mentioning that the protagonist lies to their mother in the first chapter. You could then explain that even though the protagonist is trustworthy and kind for the rest of the text, this moment shows how even good people can behave badly.

4.2 Understanding how writers create characters

Creating characters in written texts

You might remember that in literary texts, a character's appearance provides readers with clues about the character's personality and their role in the story. Paying attention to how characters look is a way of recognising, understanding and evaluating characters.

Writers make careful choices about what to focus on, so the visual details mentioned in texts are never random. The fact that a writer has mentioned something tells us that it has meaning in relation to the story, and it's your job as a reader to find or interpret that meaning.

Details about a character's appearance to look out for in texts include:

- physical build, height and colouring
- choice of clothing (including the style and colour – they might wear fashionable and expensive clothing or outdated clothes, or they might always wear a particular hat or they might frequently wear clothing that is inappropriate for the temperature or social setting)
- physical habits (including fidgeting or twitching, how slowly or quickly they usually move and whether they make eye contact with others)
- any distinctive or unusual features (including injuries, a peculiar haircut, facial hair, strange make-up or tattoos).

In literary texts, characters' appearances are conveyed primarily through written descriptions. These can include imagery and **figurative language**.

Key term

figurative language: figurative language phrases are used in non-literal ways that differ from the expected or everyday usage; examples include simile (e.g. 'white as a sheet'), metaphor (e.g. 'all the world's a stage') and personification (e.g. 'the clouds chased me')

When you read a text, collect evidence relating to the characters' physical appearances; this will help you build your understanding of the characters.

Other ways of analysing characters include focusing on:

- what they say (their dialogue) and how they say it
- the way they behave towards other characters
- their narrative journey, including how events change them and how their own decisions have consequences.

Key fact

Any *changes* to a character's appearance are important – just as changes in behaviours, relationships or settings in a text are usually meaningful. Changes are indicators that there is something significant to explore.

Activity 4.2.1

1 In your notebook or on a device, create a table like the one below for each of the main characters in a text you are studying.

Character name: Lane Jones		
Quote about the character, including page number	**What you could infer**	**Literary devices used**
'The first thing I noticed about Lane was his shifty eyes. They were always darting here and there. They were never still.' Page 38	Lane is hard to pin down and is a potentially 'shifty' person.	Repetition (the phrase 'They were ...')
'He was barely any taller standing up than sitting down.' Page 39	He is notably small, meaning he might appear powerless in some situations.	Humour (exaggeration)
'Lane never stands still, constantly jiggling like a lizard on hot sand, and usually talking a mile a minute.' Page 67	He is often uncomfortable or impatient.	Simile ('jiggling like a lizard on hot sand') and exaggeration ('a mile a minute')
'His shoelaces are untied. Again.' Page 103	He is often distracted and doesn't pay attention to small details.	Sentence fragment ('Again.') for emphasis

2 For each character, write one or two sentences summarising your opinion about them. Support your statements with references to the text.

Creating characters in visual texts

In multimodal texts that use the visual mode (e.g. images and video), visual features shape your understanding of the characters. For example, when a novel is adapted for screen, characters are created through **cinematic language**, which includes:

- costume (what the character wears, how they dress) and make-up (in genres such as fantasy, this could be full-body make-up or prosthetics)
- casting (consider characteristics the actor brings to the role, including their age, general appearance and any distinctive features)
- camera angles (consider whether the camera is above, below or alongside a character); see Table 2.12 on page 45
- props (objects or items the character uses, carries or handles)
- lighting (e.g. dim, bright, colourful, shadowy, harsh, natural or artificial).

Key term

cinematic language: the methods used to communicate with the audience visually, such as lighting, performance, costumes, ways of filming (cinematography)

Each of these aspects can help convey information about a character, either literally or symbolically. For example, if a character is always shot from a high camera angle, they may appear smaller, meaning we're likely to interpret them as having less power or less importance. If a character is usually seen in the shadows, it might suggest that they are untrustworthy or sneaky.

You're probably used to watching films and television programs and being unconsciously influenced by aspects of these visual texts. For example, black or dark clothing are frequently associated with villains, while lighter colours are often connected with characters who we're expected to like and identify with.

We can infer several things about this character by the way they are presented.

Practice noticing and recording these visual techniques. When you're watching a film or television show, ask yourself the following questions: How do you feel about particular characters? How is this shaped by the creator's choices? How does this shape the way you respond to the plot?

Think about it

Many common visual techniques, such as using dark colours to represent evil or light colours to represent innocence, have become cliches (overused or stereotyped ideas).

Think of an example in a film or television series that flips these conventions. Did you find this effective? Why or why not?

Activity 4.2.2

Imagine you're a film director who is adapting the story in which Lane Jones (from the table on page 68) appears. Use the descriptions of Lane to write a few short paragraphs explaining how you plan to portray the character. You can use the list of prompts below to help you consider your decisions.

- **What kind of film are you making (e.g. animated or live action, comedy or horror, for children or adults)?**
- **What will you need to look for in the actor playing Lane?**
- **Will you make any changes to the character described? Why might you make changes?**
- **What characteristics or elements of personality do you want to convey visually?**
- **What challenges might you anticipate in conveying this character?**

Comparing characters in written and visual texts

In English, you will be asked to compare how characters are represented in writing and on screen.

Table 4.2 shows two examples of characters in classic texts compared with their screen versions. Note how the visual representations of the characters focus on different aspects of the characters (as described in the original texts). The differences in the visual representations of the characters reflects the emotions and opinions the film creators wish to evoke in their audiences.

Table 4.2: Comparing written and visual representations of two characters

Character	The Ghost of Christmas Yet to Come from *A Christmas Carol* by Charles Dickens (this novella was published in 1843)
Quotes describing the character	'It was shrouded in a deep black garment, which concealed its head, its face, its form, and left nothing of it visible save one outstretched hand.' '... the Spirit neither spoke nor moved.'
Screen version 1 character description	• *The Muppet Christmas Carol* (1992, Disney) • The character is a puppet taller than a human; it wears a flowing grey hooded cloak, has an empty black space where the face should be and has grey stone-like skin on its huge hands

(continued)

Table 4.2: Comparing written and visual representations of two characters (continued)

Screen version 2 character description	• *A Christmas Carol* (2019, BBC) • The character appears human but with pale grey skin and very dark eyes; it wears a tall black hat and a long dress coat and its lips are stitched closed messily
Comparing the screen texts with the novel	The 1992 film presents a fairly literal visual interpretation of the character from the novel, retaining elements described by Dickens (such as the missing face). The 2019 adaptation shows us the face Dickens hides. It also draws attention to the silence Dickens identifies, by giving the spirit a dramatically sealed mouth like a character in a horror film.
Character	**The Cheshire Cat from *Alice's Adventures in Wonderland* by Lewis Carroll (this novel was published in 1865)**
Quotes describing the character	'... a large cat, which was lying on the hearth and grinning from ear to ear.' 'The Cat ... looked good-natured, she thought: still it had very long claws and a great many teeth, so she felt that it ought to be treated with respect.'
Screen version 1 character description	• *Alice in Wonderland* (1951, Disney) • The large creature has paws, ears, whiskers and yellow eyes like a cat but is otherwise cartoony and unlike a real cat; he has a huge tail, an oversized toothy grin and is striped vibrant pink and purple.
Screen version 2 character description	• *Alice in Wonderland* (2010, Disney) • The cat has highly textured, hyperreal fur but with fluorescent blue stripes; its glowing green eyes and large mouthful of crooked teeth look slightly menacing.
Comparing the screen texts with the novel	The 1951 animation, made for family audiences, portrays the Cheshire Cat as a silly, friendly creature drawn in bright colours and with an almost comical smile. This echoes the 'grin' and 'good-nature' that Lewis Carroll describes. The 2010 film, which has a much darker tone, presents the Cheshire Cat less innocently. It focuses on the mood conveyed by the 'long claws' and 'many teeth' and the fact that the creature demands 'respect'.

How literary devices and language features help create a character

Characters are more than just their appearance – to get to know them, we need to understand how they act around others, what they believe, what they desire or need and what makes them vulnerable.

Writers use language features to build and convey aspects of character, including personality traits and behaviour. Some of these features are listed in Table 4.3 on the next page.

Table 4.3: Examples of language features used to create character

Feature	Description	How it is used
Direct dialogue	What the character says	Helps us build a clearer picture of the character's personality
Register	How formally the character speaks: casually, intimately or formally	When speaking; for example, a character from a royal family will likely use formal language
Figurative language	The use of literary devices such as simile and metaphor to give a meaning that is not directly stated	Helps us imagine character details that are more abstract (such as their beliefs or fears)
Sensory imagery	Vivid details of touch, taste, smell and sound	Creates a powerful impression of a character in the reader's imagination
Visual images	Used in visual texts such as picture books and graphic novels	Visually represents a character's personality
Structure	How early or late in the text we learn important details about characters	Can influence how we feel about the character at different points in the story

Activity 4.2.3

Choose a character from a text you know well or are studying at school.

1. **Write down three features in Table 4.3 that the author has used to describe or develop the character. Add a quote showing the specific example from the text.**
2. **Write down one of the features in Table 4.3 that the author has *not* used in the text. Now use that device yourself to create a sentence helping convey more information about the character.**

How literary devices and language features influence emotions and opinions

As well as using language to create characters, writers also make careful language choices to shape the way we feel when we read a text, and to prompt us to form certain opinions about characters, settings and events. For example, the use of sensory imagery can be very powerful in manipulating our emotions. Table 4.4 lists some examples of how this can be done.

Table 4.4: How literary devices and language features might influence readers' emotions and opinions

What is being described	Description	Device used	How the description might make you feel	An opinion you might form in response
Character	When she hugged me, the scents of oranges, fresh bread and hot tea filled my nose.	Sensory imagery	Happy, nostalgic, safe, cosy	The character is kind and trustworthy.
Setting	Tino walked into the room and felt instantly chilled to the bone.	Sensory description	Cold, uneasy, uncomfortable, distrustful	The space Tino has entered is unsafe or he may be in danger.
Event	The slamming door was like a balloon bursting behind me.	Simile	Startled, shocked, scared, alert, irritated	There is tension in this scene.
Character	His parents exhausted him. His homework exhausted him. His friends exhausted him. Even his favourite games exhausted him.	Repetition	Tired, drained, hopeless, frustrated	Life as a student is overwhelming.
Setting	You would hate it if you were here: you'd want to run away, just like me.	Point of view (second person)	Empathetic, engaged, personally connected	The character shouldn't have to put up with this experience.
Event	'Quick, follow me! The train is about to leave!'	Direct dialogue	Excited, curious, motivated, energised	The situation is urgent and something significant is about to happen.

By using these features and devices, writers can influence the reader's emotional response and the opinions they form, which helps to make the story more powerful and memorable.

Activity 4.2.4

1 **In a text you are studying, find three sentences that use literary devices like the ones in the table above. For each one, write a sentence describing how the quote makes you feel.**

2 **Find another sentence in the text that uses a different literary technique but creates the same feeling.**

Examining literature

5.1 Creating meaning with characters, settings and events

Most imaginative literature tells a story using characters, settings and events. This is true for novels, short stories and plays. (Poetry is a bit different since it doesn't need to tell a story.) Western literature mainly consists of stories that are written down; literature from other traditions might be passed on through performance or the spoken word.

How authors combine characters, settings and events to create meaning

Literature tells a story through characters and events, but there is always a larger meaning. This meaning could come from the author's exploration of human qualities such as love or jealousy, or of abstract concepts such as good and evil. A message can be conveyed through the consequences of the characters' actions: 'good triumphs over evil' could be suggested by the deaths of the most violent or cruel characters, for example.

Authors also create meaning through the characters' statements, thoughts and behaviour. Readers tend to like and sympathise with characters who treat others with respect and kindness, or who demonstrate courage and loyalty. **Values** such as these are central to literature, even if they're only implied by what the characters say and do rather than being explicitly stated by a text.

Key term

values: positive qualities and aspects of human behaviour

Settings can also help to create meaning, especially through the ways that characters treat the environment or interact with it. The setting can also reflect the qualities of the person who owns or inhabits them.

For example, the following lines from Charles Dickens' *A Christmas Carol* (1843) describe both the setting of Scrooge's office and Scrooge himself.

> The door of Scrooge's counting-house was open that he might keep his eye upon his clerk, who in a dismal little cell beyond, a sort of tank, was copying letters. Scrooge had a very small fire, but the clerk's fire was so very much smaller that it looked like one coal. But he couldn't replenish it, for Scrooge kept the coal-box in his own room …

Scrooge is a moneylender who is extremely miserly and, as we learn, hates Christmas. He's well-off financially but refuses to be generous and lives alone. The office's lack of physical warmth reflects Scrooge's lack of human warmth – shown in his unkind treatment of his employee, Bob Cratchit.

In contrast to Scrooge, Cratchit is poor and has a large family, but the description of Christmas dinner at the Cratchits' home contrasts dramatically with that of Scrooge's office. The 'two tumblers, and a custard-cup' are all the glassware the family owns, but the setting suggests not deprivation but abundance.

> At last the dinner was all done, the cloth was cleared, the hearth swept, and the fire made up. The compound in the jug being tasted, and considered perfect, apples and oranges were put upon the table, and a shovel-full of chestnuts on the fire. Then all the Cratchit family drew round the hearth … and at Bob Cratchit's elbow stood the family display of glass. Two tumblers, and a custard-cup without a handle. These held the hot stuff from the jug, however, as well as golden goblets would have done; and Bob served it out with beaming looks, while the chestnuts on the fire sputtered and cracked noisily.

The meanings suggested by the characters' actions and by this setting relate to generosity, sharing and family – all things that Scrooge resists but Bob Cratchit embodies and of which the text as a whole approves. This approval is reinforced by the end of the novel, where the reformed Scrooge embraces the spirit of Christmas.

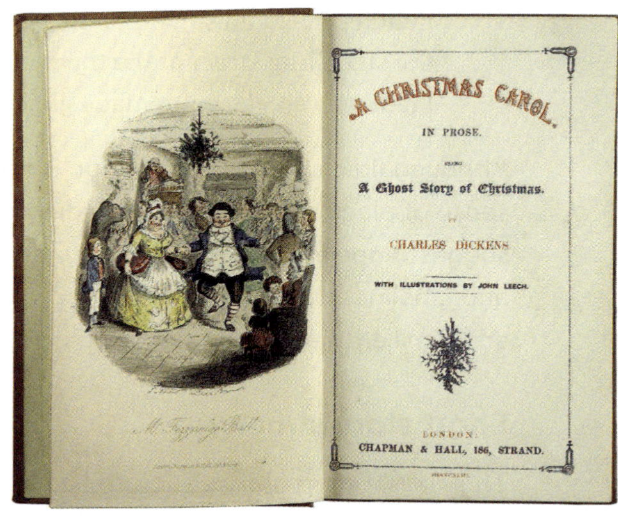

The title page of the first edition of *A Christmas Carol*, with an illustration of a ball scene – the opposite of Scrooge's idea of fun

Activity 5.1.1

Select a book you're reading, or have recently finished reading, and answer the following questions.

1. **Write down the names of three main characters. Next to each name, write two adjectives that sum up that character.**
2. **Give three words that describe a main setting. Does the author create this setting in a way that makes it appealing? Justify your answer with short quotes or examples from a passage.**

3 **Identify three of the main events in the book and explain where they occur.**

4 **What is one of the main messages or meanings you think the author would like you to get from reading this book? Explain why you think this, referring to characters, setting and events.**

Understanding short stories

A short story is a piece of prose up to about 50 pages in length. The idea is that short stories can be read in a single sitting, so they are often less than 20 pages. Because of their length, short stories generally focus on one main character and have one setting. The central character can be created in detail, while other characters are more two-dimensional.

The mood or atmosphere of a short story is very important. Authors create the mood from the start, choosing vocabulary and images carefully to achieve a particular effect. Consider these sentences from near the beginning of the short story 'A Dreamer', published in 1902 by Australian author Barbara Baynton. The protagonist has just arrived by train at a country station.

> If her letter had been received, someone would have been waiting with a buggy. She passed through the station. She saw nothing but an ownerless dog, huddled, wet and shivering, in a corner. More for sound she turned to look up the straggling street of the township. Among the sheoaks, bordering the river she knew so well, the wind made ghostly music, unheeded by the sleeping town.

Although little specific information is conveyed, the vocabulary and imagery create a sense of place as well as a foreboding mood. The adjectives 'straggling' and 'ghostly' suggest hopelessness, while the image of the dog captures feelings of unhappiness and loneliness. It's clear that the protagonist is anxiously searching for reassurance and familiarity, and this search is the source of the tension that runs through the story.

Short story structures

The classic short story structure has the tension rising steadily to a climax, then falling as the conflict is resolved (see the diagram on page 18). However, many authors vary this. For instance, some short stories don't have a lot of tension or conflict. Others do have conflict but they don't resolve the conflict at the end, leaving the reader in a state of suspense. Sometimes a twist at the end takes the reader by surprise.

Another way authors can vary the structure is by describing events out of order. Often the narrative will begin with the earliest event and describe what happens in chronological order. But sometimes the author varies the order of events to create more interest and suspense.

For example, a story might begin **in medias res**, then backtrack to earlier events before bringing the reader up to date and then describing what happens next to resolve the conflict. Or the author might use a **circular structure** by beginning with the most recent event, then going back to the start and describing everything that happened up to the present.

A **frame narrative** is another structure occasionally used for short stories, although it is more common in longer narratives such as novels and films. The narrator introduces the main story which might be narrated by another character, or consist of a different text such as a letter.

Key terms

in medias res: beginning in the middle of the action

circular structure: where the author begins with the most recent event, then goes back to the earliest event and describes everything leading up to the point at which the story began

frame narrative: the literary device of telling a story within a story

Activity 5.1.2

Answer these questions for a short story you've read or are studying in class.

1. **Summarise the plot in three sentences.**
2. **How does the author set the scene in the opening paragraphs? What mood is created, and what word choices and images help create this mood?**
3. **What structure is used for the story? Is it chronological, in medias res, circular or something else?**
4. **What is the central problem or conflict that keeps the reader interested right to the end of the story?**

Understanding other storytelling traditions

Many storytelling traditions aren't written down. They might be entirely oral (spoken), or they might draw on existing stories (such as myths, legends or folklore) and retell them in ways that rely on oral or visual language. In Australia, First Nations peoples have storytelling traditions in which stories are performed using actions, dance, body painting and music. In Japan, Noh drama is a popular traditional form of storytelling that relies heavily on masks and gestures. On the Indonesian islands of Java and Bali, the puppet theatre tradition of wayang tells stories using illuminated puppets placed behind a screen, so that the audience sees the shadows of the puppets. The puppets' movements and dialogue are enhanced by singing and instrumental music.

In wayang, the puppeteer, or dalang, moves the puppets and performs the dialogue of the characters.

Activity 5.1.3

Select a storytelling tradition that relies mainly on the spoken word, rather than the written word. It can involve visual elements and music or just be an oral performance. Summarise its main features and analyse how the aspects that are non-verbal (not using words) contribute to the story being told and the meanings being created.

5.2 Creating meaning with literary devices

How authors use literary devices

As discussed in earlier chapters, a literary device is a strategy or technique a writer uses to make readers think or feel a certain way about a character, relationship, event or situation. Have you ever tried to explain something by comparing it to something else? You might have been using a literary device such as an analogy or a simile – a comparison that highlights the similarities between two things, like your bedroom and a tip!

Some common literary devices are shown in Table 5.1. (We already looked at some of these in relation to poetry in Chapter 2 – see page 51).

Table 5.1: Common literary devices

Device	Definition
Allusion	A reference to another literary work or well-known person, place or thing
Foreshadowing	Hinting at something that's going to happen
Imagery	Visually descriptive or figurative language to represent objects, actions, ideas and so on in ways that appeal to the senses of a reader or viewer
Juxtaposition	Where two things are placed beside each other to emphasise their differences
Metaphor	A comparison where one thing is described as something else
Personification	To give living qualities to a non-living thing
Repetition	The use of the same sound, word, phrase or sentence multiple times
Simile	A comparison where one thing is described as being similar to something else, using the words 'like' or 'as'
Symbolism	The use of an object to represent something else, often an abstract idea or concept

Key understanding

Some literary devices can appear in any text type. For example, you can find similes in novels, short stories, plays, poems and nonfiction texts. But some literary devices are associated with particular kinds of texts. For example, rhyme is mostly used in poetry and exaggeration is most often used in humorous or persuasive texts.

How authors use literary devices to create meaning

Authors don't use literary devices randomly. They use them to communicate important ideas or to evoke particular emotions in readers. One of the characteristics of a literary text is the writer's skilful use of literary devices to create particular effects.

Consider the examples from JRR Tolkien's *The Hobbit* in Table 5.2. The novel tells the story of Bilbo Baggins, whose peaceful life drastically changes when the wizard Gandalf pushes him to accompany a group of dwarves on a quest.

Table 5.2: Some common literary devices that are used in *The Hobbit*

Device	Example and effect
Allusion	Tolkien makes many allusions to Norse, Celtic and Anglo-Saxon language and mythology; for example, the runes on Thrór's map are based on Old English runes.
Foreshadowing	Gandalf says about Bilbo, 'There is a lot more in him than you guess, a deal more than he has any idea of himself', foreshadowing the ways Bilbo will be tested and grow on his journey.
Imagery	In Mirkwood Forest, Bilbo sees 'a place of dense black shadow ahead of him, black even for that forest, like a patch of midnight that had never been cleared away', emphasising the mystery and danger of the place.
Juxtaposition	Bilbo's safe, happy home in the Shire is juxtaposed with the much more dangerous but also more exciting world beyond it.
Metaphor	Smaug the dragon tells Bilbo, 'my teeth are swords, my claws spears, the shock of my tail a thunderbolt, my wings a hurricane, and my breath death!', painting a frightening image.
Personification	The description of a beautiful day includes the phrase 'the sun dancing on the water', evoking a sense of joy.
Repetition	Gandalf responds to Bilbo wishing him good morning with 'Do you wish me a good morning, or mean that it is a good morning whether I want it or not; or that you feel good this morning; or that it is a morning to be good on?', revealing his challenging and complex character.
Simile	Smaug is described as emitting 'a sort of bubbling like the noise of a large pot galloping on the fire, mixed with a rumble as of a gigantic tom-cat purring', vivid comparisons that convey his size and threat.
Symbolism	In the story, the ring is an important symbol, showing the appeal and the corrupting effect of power.

Activity 5.2.1

1 Identify the literary devices used in each of the examples below.

a The dumpsite was a mountain range of rubbish, stretching as far as the eye could see.

b The weight of the crown they placed on her head made her neck and shoulders ache – she had never asked for this.

c I love writing, though I'm no Shakespeare!

2 Read the two paragraphs below and answer the questions that follow.

The bells chimed, setting the sparrows soaring, and it was clear the celebration of Harvesttime was coming to the city of Raneiris, golden-rooved by the river. The sand-brick houses were joyous with colourful streamers. Down alleys and painted laneways, wending past spindly trees and pots trailing with red geraniums, past the bustling marketplace, past the butter-yellow-paved town square, the happy crowd trailed. Most were in high spirits, singing out their chants with full voice like a chorus of cardinals. The children were sparrows, jumping and darting through legs and underfoot, occasionally called back by a worried parent.

...

In a vault deep underground, lurking under the glimmering grandeur of Raneiris, there is a safe. It is locked, covered with a heavy velvet blanket, tucked behind a dusty bookshelf. A thin shaft of light peeks through cracks in the vault's ancient doorway, enough to illuminate the dingy surrounds.

a **Underline one simile.**

b **Circle one example of imagery.**

c **Highlight a repeated word or phrase.**

d **Complete the following sentence:**
The writer uses juxtaposition when they contrast ________________ with ______________. This makes the reader feel _____________________ and think ____________.

e **A cardinal is a bright red songbird. Write a sentence explaining what the phrase 'singing out their chants with full voice like a chorus of cardinals' is intended to make the reader think about the crowd's chanting.**

How to understand literary devices in poetry

Poets use literary devices like metaphors and similes just as novelists and short story writers do. In Chapter 2, we looked at some common poetic techniques, including alliteration and metaphor. But because poetry is intended to be heard, not just read, poets will also use poetic techniques to create the **sounds** and **rhythms** that make poetry different from other forms of writing. Some of the devices poets use are in Table 5.3.

Table 5.3: Common literary devices used in poetry

Device	Definition
Alliteration	Use of the same sounds at the starts of words
End rhyme	Similar sounds at the ends of two or more lines of poetry
Enjambment	When a sentence or phrase extends beyond the end of a line or verse into the next without a pause or punctuation mark
Internal rhyme	Similar sounds at the end of two of words within a line of poetry
Metre	The pattern of beats in a line of poetry, created by stressed syllables and unstressed syllables
Punctuation	The use of marks such as full stops, commas and exclamation marks to control pace and rhythm in a poem

Key terms

stressed syllables: units of sound that would be emphasised if read aloud

unstressed syllables: units of sound that would not be emphasised if read aloud

The poem below was written by nineteenth-century poet Edward Lear, who was well known for his humorous, sometimes nonsensical rhymes. The annotations point out some of the poetic devices he uses.

Said the Duck to the Kangaroo 'Good gracious! How you hop!	The poem uses a non-standard **metre** (stressed syllables underlined), to create a rhythm similar to a kangaroo's hop. The alliterative expressions help to create the wistful but humorous voice of the Duck.
Over the fields and the water too, As if you never would stop!	Punctuation with multiple exclamation marks creates the Duck's character and voice, and the poem's excited tone.
My life is a bore in this nasty pond And I long to go out in the world beyond!	End rhyme is used in every second line of the first half of the **stanza**, creating musicality and contributing to the even rhythm. This changes to rhyming couplets in the second half, creating a more wistful tone.
I wish I could hop like you!' Said the Duck to the Kangaroo.	The words 'long' and 'beyond' create a close internal rhyme within this line that emphasises the Duck's strong feelings.

Notice how the use of poetic devices allows Lear to build up layers of meaning in his poem. The basic idea expressed in this stanza is that a duck envies a kangaroo's ability to hop. But Lear's choices about which words to use and how to arrange them communicate larger themes and ideas. The jaunty rhythm echoes the Kangaroo's gait and has associations with joy, ease and freedom. The use of exclamatory statements and internal and end rhymes suggest that the Duck feels trapped and that his wish to be like the Kangaroo, although powerful, is futile.

Activity 5.2.2

1 Do you think the Duck's wish to hop like the Kangaroo is foolish or understandable? What do you believe Lear wants us to think? Why do you think this?

2 Write an annotation identifying a poetic device and its effect in the haiku below.

> Drifting dusk descends.
> A white apparition waits
> to meet with the crowd.

3 Write your own poem, choosing an element from each row of the following table.

Title	'The witching hour'	'Dream delayed'	'The search'
Symbol	Bird	Red scarf	Skyscraper
Imagery	Fading like fingerprints on an icy window	Still, suffocating silence	Seeds that might one day flower
Rhyme pattern	ABAB (every second line rhymes)	AABB (pairs of lines rhyme)	No rhyme

Understanding imagery in First Nations stories

Look at the First Nations imagery below. What do the images make you think of?

The art and storytelling of many First Nations language groups in Australia use symbols like these to represent the tracks of different animals. There are many different First Nations language groups, each with their own distinct ways of using symbols and imagery. Animals and nature are two important elements of First Nations storytelling, often used to present complex ideas. For example, a story from Yirrkala in the Northern Territory tells how a boy who ate all the fish intended for his family group was turned into a seagull – a warning against greed.

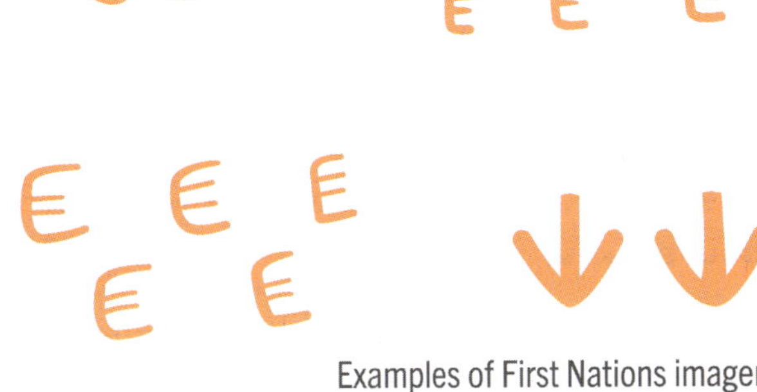

Examples of First Nations imagery

Activity 5.2.3

1 **Bunjil (the wedge-tailed eagle) is the creator and protector of the environment for the people of the Kulin Nation in south-central Victoria. Do some research into stories about Bunjil. What are three adjectives you would use to describe him?**

2 **Choose one of the adjectives you came up with in Question 1 and create a vivid simile, metaphor or unique description of Bunjil that includes the adjective.**

A wedge-tailed eagle

How to evaluate a literary text

What's your favourite book or film? What do you love about it? Is there a text you've read or viewed that you really *didn't* like? Why?

We all make judgements about texts every day. But as we learned in Chapter 1, evaluating a text means doing more than just stating a personal opinion about your enjoyment of it. When you're assessing the value of a literary text, you need to think about the qualities that make a successful text of that type. Sometimes you might come across texts that you don't personally enjoy, but which you believe are 'good' or successful texts anyway.

We often talk about literary texts having **aesthetic** value. This is a quality that sets them apart from other texts, such as newspaper articles, social media posts and advertisements, which we don't usually consider 'literary'. But what does it mean to have aesthetic value? You might have heard 'aesthetic' used to describe the appearance or mood of a place or thing. In terms of literary texts, it means thinking about a text's:

- beauty – its language, style and structure
- ability to stir readers' emotions.

Key term

aesthetic: to do with beauty or concerning the appreciation of beauty

So what sorts of questions might you ask yourself to decide the value of a literary text? Try these:

- Has the writer used language in interesting, original ways?
- Is the text pleasurable to read? If you were to read it aloud, would the words and sentences create a pleasant rhythm?
- What messages or ideas is the writer communicating? Are these interesting or important?
- Does the form of the text help the writer to communicate their ideas?

Remember that any written evaluations you make of a text always need to be supported by evidence from the text.

Activity 5.2.4

1. **Identify one text you think would be classified as a literary text and one that you think would not. Explain the differences between the two. What makes the literary text literary?**
2. **Rewrite the following social media post as a paragraph from a literary novel.**

   'Great time at the beach with the gang today!'

Understanding film adaptations of literature

Many popular movies are based on well-loved novels. Some you might know are *The Lord of the Rings* series, *Paddington* and *Charlie and the Chocolate Factory*. Because film is a visual medium, filmmakers can use actors, cinematography, editing and computer-generated imagery (CGI) to communicate ideas in new ways. Adapting novels into films also allows stories to reach new audiences.

But there are challenges for filmmakers too. Long or complicated narratives often need to be condensed for film. Capturing the mood and tone created by the language of a beloved novel in a film script can also be tricky.

Fun fact

Some stories are so well loved that they get retold in multiple ways and in different formats. You might know the 2024 film *Wicked*, starring Ariana Grande and Cynthia Erivo. But did you know that the film is based on the first act of a 2003 stage musical by Winnie Holzman and Stephen Schwartz? They based the play on a 1995 novel by Gregory Maguire, who in turn drew on L Frank Baum's 1900 novel *The Wonderful Wizard of Oz*, as well as the 1939 movie with the same name. Clearly, the characters and story have had a lasting impact!

The Princess Bride is another popular film that was adapted from a novel (by William Goldman, 1973). It is a fairytale about Princess Buttercup and farm boy Westley, who fall in love. Although Goldman wrote both the novel and the film script, there are quite a few differences between the two versions of the story. Some of the main ones are summarised below:

- **The frame narrative:** Both the book and the film involve a man reading a story to a young boy in the 'real' world. The main story of Buttercup and Westley, set in the imaginary world of Florin, is the story that he reads. But in the book, this frame narrative is more complicated and detailed. The father reading the book to his son is a version of the author, William Goldman, who claims his novel is a retelling of a (fictional) book his own father read to him as a child with the boring bits left out.
- **The character of Buttercup:** In the novel, Princess Buttercup is depicted as a bit slow or stupid. But in the film, she is clever and daring.
- **The action scenes:** In the novel, the fights between various characters include long descriptions, while the film uses rapid cuts and choreographed action to make them exciting and fast paced.
- **The use of flashbacks:** The novel includes more flashbacks and fills in the backstories of some characters more than the movie does.

You can probably guess why some of these changes were made. It would be harder to explain on screen the complicated situation of the author William Goldman, his fictional father who read him the story of *The Princess Bride* when he was young and his rewriting this story to make it more interesting for own son. Long descriptions of action in a book can be depicted much faster visually. It's also common for minor characters in a novel or elements of characters' backstories to be cut out of the film version if they are not essential to the plot.

The Venn diagram on the next page shows some vocabulary that is associated with novels and some with film. The centre of the diagram includes terms associated with both novels and films.

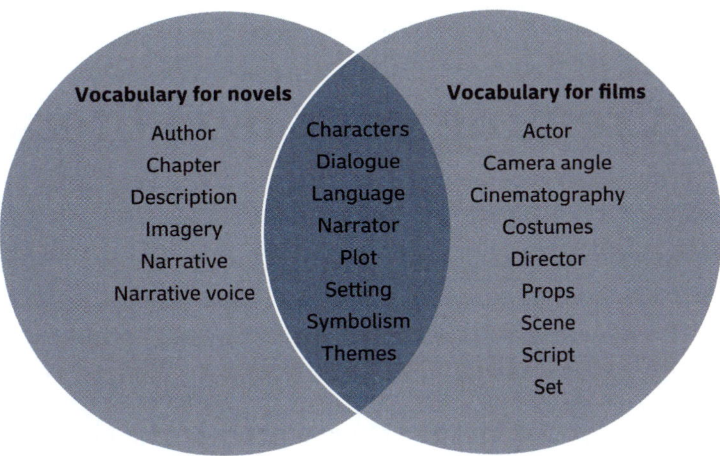

A Venn diagram of vocabulary for novels and films

Understanding valuable verbs

Using strong and precise verbs in your writing about texts will help you to communicate your meaning clearly and concisely. Some useful verbs for writing about the process of adapting a novel for the screen include the following.

adapt	amend	create	complicate	extend
position	recreate	revise	simplify	transform

Activity 5.2.5

1 **Look up definitions of any of the words above that are unfamiliar.**

2 **Why do you think the character of Buttercup was written to be smarter in *The Princess Bride* film than in the book? Do you think the film would be so popular if the main female character was depicted as not very smart? Why or why not?**

3 **What are some advantages of telling a story in print?**

4 **What are some ways films can convey information or ideas more easily than the written word?**

Creating your own literature

6.1 Experimenting with your writing

In the Literature section, you've looked at how authors create high-quality works of fiction. You've examined how they use language features and literary devices in their writing, how context affects what they have to say and how you can evaluate their work by studying the features of what they've created.

The next part of studying literature is to think about creating your own works of fiction, putting what you've studied into practice to help take your writing to the next level.

This chapter examines some of the creative tasks you might be asked to do as part of Year 7 English. We'll describe what's required by the task and how you can approach it.

Imaginative re-creations

An imaginative re-creation involves taking an already created artistic work and imagining it in a new way.

Think back to the story 'The Drover's Wife', discussed in Chapter 3. Writer–director Leah Purcell took a simple story that she had loved as a child and reimagined it as a tale of a First Nations woman fighting for her family. This broadens the scope of the original story and gives it new meaning.

Imaginative re-creations can also be a lot of fun. As a writer, you can start with a character or situation you already know and ask, 'What if?' What if Katniss Everdeen from *The Hunger Games* had to live with your family? What if Harry Potter decided to try to join Lord Voldemort? What if Cinderella lived in modern times and decided to get revenge on everyone who had wronged her? As you can see, thinking this way can open up a lot of interesting possibilities.

How to approach an imaginative re-creation

1. Decide on the original text or character you want to reimagine. Write down the main features that you would want to keep in a new situation.
2. Decide how you will reimagine the text. Will you move a single character to a new location or situation and see how they react? Or do you want to move the whole story? For example, you could take the character of Little Red Riding Hood and write about how she would react if she were lost in a big, modern city.

Or you could move the whole story of Little Red Riding Hood so that she now must deliver medicine to her grandmother in a forbidding city apartment block, and where there is a big, bad bully instead of a Big Bad Wolf.

3. Consider whether your characters will know they have come from another place/story or whether they've just been 'dropped in' and don't know what is happening.
4. Think about how the character or characters will behave in a new setting. Is there any way the new situation would change them? You want the character to be consistent across the texts, but you also want to let the new situation create interesting predicaments.
5. Finally, decide how you'll resolve the story. Will your character go back to their original setting? Will they decide to stay? Or are they stuck?!

Creating a prequel

A **prequel** is a story that shows the events that happen before those of an existing work. For example, the film *Rogue One* is a prequel to *Star Wars: A New Hope*. It's set one week before the events of the latter film and involves characters that are mentioned only in passing in the original film.

Similar to an imaginative re-creation, a prequel involves reimagining a character in a new setting or situation. However, a prequel also involves describing the events or decisions that lead up to the start of the original work. It gives the reader or viewer new insight into the original.

Because a prequel starts before an existing text, you'll need to work backwards from the start of the original to create your piece. For example, if we wanted to write a prequel to the story of Little Red Riding Hood, we would need to show how Little Red Riding Hood's grandmother becomes ill, how Little Red Riding Hood realises she needs to help her and how the Big Bad Wolf becomes so hungry.

Key term

prequel: a story that shows the events that happen before those of an existing work

How to approach creating a prequel

1. Decide on the original text you want to make a prequel to. This can be a film, show or written narrative.
2. Note down where your story will need to end, including where each character has to end up. Then think about how you will make that happen. This is another situation where you can have some fun. Continuing our Little Red Riding Hood example, perhaps her grandmother was a mad scientist who ate some

chemicals. Perhaps Little Red Riding Hood is a sulky teenager who really doesn't want to help anyone. And maybe the Big Bad Wolf has been trying to go vegetarian, which is what has made him so hungry.

3 Create an outline to guide your writing. You need to have a clear structure that will take your characters up to the point where the original work starts. This will be the end of your piece.

One of the suggestions from the curriculum involves presenting your prequel as a scripted monologue. A **monologue** is a long speech by one actor in a play or film. If you're asked to do this, have your character reflect on the events in their life. You might include flashbacks – scenes where they remember something that happened but are describing it as if it were happening now.

Key term

monologue: a long speech by one actor in a play or film

Key fact

A flashback is a way to show action that took place before the main events of the story. Flashbacks can give the reader or viewer background information or shed light on why a character does something or feels a certain way. An effective flashback should move the story forward in some way. The reader should feel immersed in it, but it should also be clear to them where they are in the story.

Experimenting with narrative structures

We've touched on common narrative structures in Chapter 1. Once you understand the basic framework of a narrative, you can then play around with the form of what you're writing.

Some ways to play around with narrative structure include writing in **epistolary** or diary form and using multiple narrators.

Key term

epistolary: in the form of letters

Epistolary writing

Epistolary writing is just a fancy way of saying your piece is written like letters sent back and forth between characters, as a series of diary entries or as digital communication such as emails or chat messages. This can be a playful way to approach a piece of writing. Famous examples include Bram Stoker's *Dracula* and Helen Fielding's *Bridget Jones's Diary*. A more modern example is Calvin Kasulke's *Several People Are Typing*, in which a whole novel is written as a series of group chats between office workers.

Using this approach requires careful planning. You'll still need to follow a narrative arc, where the letters your characters write set the scene, deal with an issue or conflict, then come to a resolution.

You will also need to plan out your characters – not just who they are, but also how they use letters, diary entries or digital communication to tell their story. Will you have two characters writing back and forth? Or one character recounting the story in a diary or blog? Or will you have a child writing to or messaging their future self?

Don't forget to clarify your setting, tone and themes. These are still important in an epistolary narrative.

Using multiple narrators

Writing with multiple narrators means each chapter or section has a different character telling a different scene in the story. (Or sometimes different characters telling the same scene but from different points of view.)

This technique can add a lot of interest to a story. For example, the young adult novel *One of Us Is Lying* uses multiple narrators to build suspense around a murder mystery. Five high school students enter detention, but only four make it out alive. Each of those four students tells parts of the story from their perspective, and each of them is a suspect. But as we learn different things from different characters, the reader is kept guessing.

If you use this writing technique, you really must have the **voices** of your characters clear. As well as planning out the story itself, you'll need to plan out each character, how they will move the story forward and how you'll make them sound distinct. You might even want to go as far as writing down different words each of them would use.

Activity 6.1.1

Choose one of the suggested kinds of creative writing from this chapter and write a one-page story.

Activity 6.1.2

Go back over the creative piece you wrote for Activity 6.1.1 or find another creative piece you have written, and see how you can make your writing more literary.

1. **Look at your descriptions. Add sensory imagery (taste, touch, smell etc.) to some of them.**
2. **Find where you have described something and see if you can add alliteration. For example, make a tall character a 'tall, towering giant', or make an office look 'clean and clinical'.**
3. **Have you used any similes? For example, something as big as a house or as free as a bird? See if you can turn one or two of your similes into metaphors instead; for example, instead of saying 'Abdi was as free as a bird', change to 'Abdi was a bird; he leapt and swept, and swung about, his limbs flying and free.' (If you don't have any similes, add some of those in too!)**
4. **Sprinkle in some 'wow' words. While you don't want your story crammed with over-the-top words, a few interesting word choices will help to make your writing exciting. For example, you could say something was small, but it might be more engaging to use the word 'miniscule'. Or take a 'boring' day and make it 'tedious and interminable'.**
5. **Finally, edit your writing, making sure you have applied grammar and punctuation rules. Chapter 11 provides specific guidance on how to edit your own work, but for now apply what you already know – capital letters, end punctuation and so on.**

Activity 6.1.3

Reimagine a written story as a short film. Write some notes about how you would adapt it, and if you have time, try to film some of your ideas.

PART 3 LITERACY

Interacting with others – speaking and listening

7.1 Sharing ideas and information

Throughout high school, you will be required to deliver spoken presentations or be involved in discussions or debates with the aim of informing, entertaining or persuading your peers and teachers. Giving spoken presentations or contributing effectively to class discussions can sometimes be scary, but communication is a skill like any other – you can improve it with practice.

Speaking and listening

How comfortable are you in expressing your opinion? Maybe it depends on the situation, and who you're speaking with. There are two main sorts of speaking you might be asked to do in your English classes: **informal discussions** and **formal presentations**.

Key terms

informal discussion: also known as class contributions; a spoken discussion that doesn't require much preparation

formal presentation: a spoken presentation that you're expected to write and rehearse ahead of time

Whichever sort of oral communication you're doing, there are some basic principles that will help you to express your thoughts clearly and listen to the ideas of others thoughtfully. Some of the most important are summarised in Table 7.1.

Table 7.1: Speaking and listening skills

Speaking	• **Voice:** Use your voice purposefully. Pay attention to your volume and tone so that the sound of your voice supports your ideas. • **Eye contact:** Make eye contact with your listeners to build a connection and encourage them to listen. • **Pause:** Think before you speak. Even in spontaneous discussions, you'll express yourself more clearly if you take a moment to think about what you want to say before you say it. • **Order:** Try to order what you say so it makes your point clear. • **Address your audience:** Ask direct questions, use inclusive language like 'we' and 'us', and tag questions like 'isn't it?' and 'aren't they?'
Listening	• **Body language:** Use facial expressions and body language to indicate you're listening. For example, nod, smile and sit up straight. • **Eye contact:** Make eye contact with the speaker to show you're listening and help them feel comfortable. • **Pay attention:** Not only is this an essential aspect of polite discussion, it's also helpful if you need to reply to or rebut others' ideas. • **Repeat:** If taking part in a discussion, repeat or rephrase what a classmate has said to check your understanding. • **Ask:** Asking questions will show interest in what the speaker is saying and develop your own knowledge of the topic.

We'll look more closely at some of these communication principles in later sections of this chapter.

Understanding classroom etiquette

Much of the advice in this chapter is based on the idea of classroom etiquette. This means speaking politely, avoiding aggressive or offensive language, and listening respectfully to the ideas of others rather than rejecting them immediately or acting bored. Essentially, when it comes to class interactions, treat others how you'd like to be treated and you can't go too wrong!

Activity 7.1.1

1 **Work with a partner for this activity. Take it in turns to give your opinion on a text you have studied in class. Ask your partner at least two questions to clarify your understanding and show your interest in their opinion.**

2 **In your discussion with your partner, how well do you think you demonstrated the skills summarised in Table 7.1? Identify one skill from each row you think you did well and one from each row that you could improve on.**

Speaking formally

One of the most common types of oral presentations you will do in English is a formal presentation to your teacher and the whole class. You might be explaining an unfamiliar topic, analysing a text or presenting a point of view on an issue.

The following guidelines will help you to prepare and deliver an effective formal presentation, whatever your purpose.

- **Make sure you're familiar with the marking key and task requirements** for your spoken presentation. Ask your teacher if you're not sure. Pay special attention to how long you're expected to speak.
- **Plan the structure of your talk** (e.g. 'in paragraph one, I'll talk about …', 'in paragraph two, I'll talk about …' etc.) before you start writing.
- **Begin with an interesting hook** (such as a fact, anecdote, question or joke) that will help to engage your audience immediately.
- **Focus on three main points or ideas** and develop these points with evidence, details and examples. If your talk is about a text, include direct quotes from the text. If your speech is about an issue, you may need to do some research to find evidence.
- **Use appropriately formal language** – this doesn't mean you need to sound artificially stiff or use overly complex language. But you should be precise and clear. Avoid slang or very casual language.
- **Finish with a bang!** Leave your audience thinking with a powerful closing statement.

Key fact

Speaking at a rate of around 120 words per minute will enable your audience to clearly follow your speech. This means that a four-minute presentation would be around 480 words.

Palm cards and visual aids

Sometimes you'll be permitted to deliver a spoken presentation using palm cards or visual aids, such as posters or slide presentations. The main thing to remember when using materials like this is that they need to support your presentation and not be a distraction to you or the audience. Some tips for using palm cards and visual aids are listed in Table 7.2.

Table 7.2: Palm cards and visual aids

Palm cards	Visual aids
• Include only brief phrases, dot points or single words to trigger your memory, rather than full sentences. • Number the palm cards in case they get out of order. • Don't panic if you lose your place. Take a deep breath and calmly review your cards until you find your place. • Maintain eye contact with your audience, only glancing at your palm cards occasionally. • Make cards that fit in the palm of your hands (about 5 × 8 cm). • Use cardboard, not paper, as it's sturdier and therefore easier to hold and to transition from one to the other.	• Visual aids should be engaging and colourful but avoid over-cluttering. • Ensure that the visual aids are used to support your spoken elements rather than distract from them. • Keep written text to a minimum; too much can be overwhelming and off-putting for an audience. • Ensure that any written or visual elements are an appropriate size so the audience can read/see them. • Costumes and props can help you 'get into character' or adopt the persona of someone else, but make sure these are appropriate and don't distract the audience from listening to you.

Stand and deliver

After you've written your presentation comes the scary part – you need to deliver it to your audience. Try the tips in Table 7.3.

Table 7.3: Voice and body language guidelines

Voice	Body language
• Vary the pitch of your voice and use volume and emphasis to draw attention to important points. • Make sure the tone of your voice is appropriate to the subject matter and the emotions you want your audience to feel. • Slow down. Pauses are important to allow your audience to absorb your point. (You could write 'PAUSE' in appropriate places on palm cards to remind you.) • Don't make sentences too long or you may find yourself running out of breath.	• Look directly at your listeners as often as possible. • Use gestures (such as pointing, lifting your hands and so on) for emphasis and visual interest. • Think about your posture and facial expressions – be positive and engaging. • Your conclusion is the most important part – know it off by heart so that you can look at the audience as you deliver it.

Always remember the two Ps of effective formal oral presentations – Preparation and Practice!

Your body language and eye contact create a connection between you and your audience.

Activity 7.1.2

1 **Highlight the phrases below that would be appropriate for a formal oral presentation.**

I'd like to begin by ...

Hey guys.

Listen up!

There is evidence to support my point.

Only an idiot would disagree.

2 **For all the phrases you didn't choose in Question 1, rewrite them to be appropriately formal.**

Making yourself heard – speaking informally

Not all your oral contributions in class will be formal. You'll often be involved in class discussions, conversations in pairs or small groups, impromptu debates and so on that allow you to speak informally.

Not everyone finds it easy to express their opinions in a group situation. Some things to keep in mind include the following:

- **Signal what you're going to say** before launching into a long explanation. For example, if you're having a class discussion about a theme in a text, you might begin by saying, 'I'd like to say something about how character X connects to that idea.' Then explain your point.
- **Signpost the reasons or points** in your contribution. This will make it easier to follow your ideas. You can do this by using words and phrases such as 'first', 'second', 'third' and 'finally'.
- **Use simple, direct sentences** as often as possible – this makes it easier to express your ideas, and for others to understand them.
- **Respond to others directly** by commenting on their contributions and asking questions to encourage them to expand on their ideas. If you're an active listener, hopefully your classmates will behave the same when you're speaking!
- **Take turns** – everyone in the pair, small group or class that you're working with should have the same opportunity to share their ideas. So don't dominate the

discussion (no matter how well-informed your opinion might be!). But also don't hesitate to raise your hand, speak up or respond to others to make sure you're claiming your fair share of speaking time.

In all our verbal interactions with others, we rely on our voice to communicate meaning and achieve our purposes. This is as true for informal spoken interactions as it is for formal presentations. For example, we might slow the pace of our speaking and increase our volume when we want someone to listen to an important point we're trying to make, or we may soften the tone of our voice to show sympathy for someone.

Understanding rebuttal

Rebuttal is the act of replying to an argument in a debate with an opposing response. Being a good listener doesn't mean you always have to agree with others. An important part of any discussion is debating ideas. Just make sure you do so respectfully. You could use phrases like: 'I agree with you about X but I have to disagree about Y', 'I respectfully disagree because …' and 'I understand what you're saying, but have you thought about …'. As always, make sure you support your opinion with reasons and evidence.

Activity 7.1.3

Imagine you're part of a class debate on the topic 'Primary school students should not have homework'.

- **Brainstorm some arguments either for or against (i.e. agree or disagree). Prepare palm cards with at least three major points in support of your opinion.**
- **Practise presenting your argument either in front of a friendly audience or, if you are at home, with a recording device such as a phone. Note how many times you say 'um' or 'ah' or if you are fidgeting or not looking at the audience. Try again, practising to make your presentation flow more smoothly.**

Identifying evidence in spoken arguments

A common task in English study is to examine an argument to identify how a writer or speaker is trying to persuade their audience to agree with their point of view.

To do this effectively, you need to 'pull apart' the argument to figure out how it has been put together, like taking apart an electronic device to see how it works. For example, if you were analysing a debate between two speakers, you would need to identify each speaker's main contention, their reasons and then the evidence used to support those reasons.

Consider the example opposite, which summarises the argument presented by a guest speaker at a school assembly. The speaker aims to persuade their audience to support introducing a mandatory test for Australians who want to own a pet.

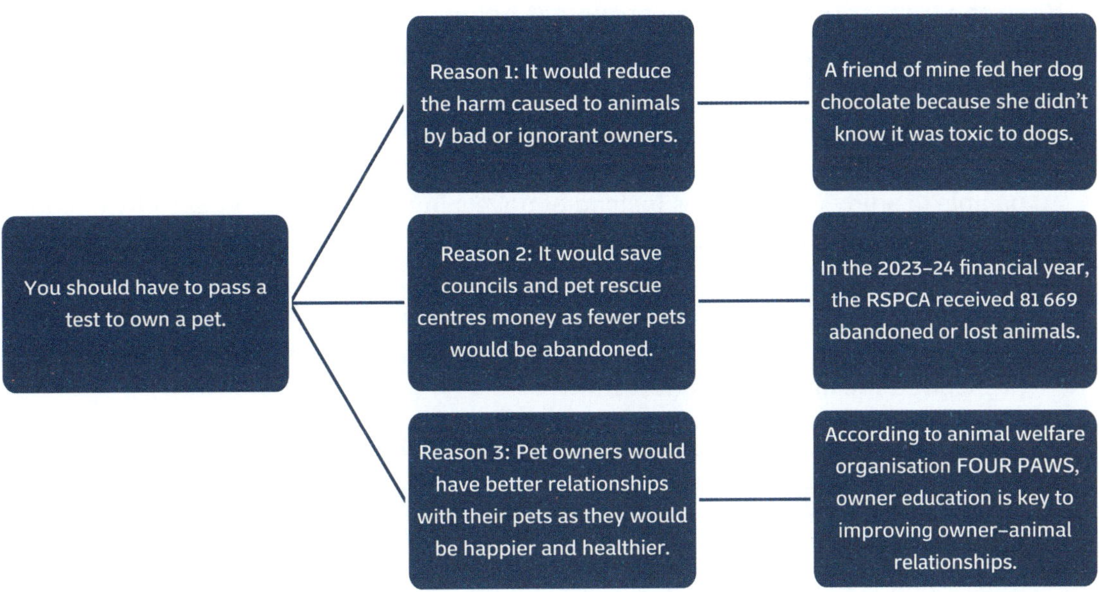

Example of a spoken argument for introducing a mandatory test for Australians who want to own a pet

A strong argument will always be supported by strong reasons and reliable evidence. Types of evidence include:

- facts
- statistics
- expert opinion
- personal experience.

The person speaking about pet ownership presents several different types of evidence to support their view, including personal experience, a statistic and expert opinion.

Understanding evidence

Effective arguments include different types of evidence, rather than just one type. For example, an argument only supported by statistics is likely to be pretty dry and dull, while an argument supported only by personal experiences might not be reliable.

Activity 7.1.4

1 Create a diagram like the one about pet ownership, presenting the other side of the argument; that is, that people should *not* be required to pass a test to own a pet. Give three clear reasons for your view, and support each reason with a different type of evidence.

2 Read the transcript of a spoken argument below. Highlight each speaker's main contention, circle the reasons and underline the evidence used to support those reasons.

Levi: I reckon *Battle Celestial* might be the best game I've ever played. We should be able to study video games instead of novels in English class. Engaged students learn better – Ms Singh always says so.

Aliya: No way. Video games aren't literature. Literature needs to explore big ideas. I've played a lot of games and none have made me feel the same emotions or inspired me like a good novel can.

Levi: I disagree. I could write 10 essays about the themes in *Battle Celestial.* I read an article about a school that taught video games as texts, and apparently students' literacy skills improved by an average of 10 per cent.

Aliya: Sounds impressive. But, sorry, I still don't believe we should study games as literature. Writers like Charlotte Brontë and Charles Dickens have been studied in English classes for years – you can't say the same about game creators.

Choosing the right language for your audience

The way we interact with others is influenced by who they are and why we are interacting with them. There are many kinds of **audiences** and **purposes**. Your audience might be people of a particular age. They may be from a specific location or cultural group. You may know them very well or they may be strangers. Your purpose might be to entertain, convince or inform. In interactions such as spoken presentations, we might speak differently or use different language to achieve our purpose and engage our audience.

Imagine you're at a job interview. Your audience members are the interviewers, and your purpose is to convince them that you're the right candidate for the job. You should speak clearly and at a steady pace so you seem professional, and so the interviewer can understand you. You're probably sitting close to the interviewers in a quiet environment, so you should talk at a regular volume. The tone created by your language choices should be serious and sincere, and your tone of voice should be calm and controlled.

Now imagine that you're telling a funny story to a group of friends. The audience is a large group of people you know well, and your purpose is to entertain them. Your volume should be louder than usual so that the large group can hear you. Your tone of voice is likely to be exaggerated to communicate the drama and emotions of your story. You can be playful with many features of voice for comedic effect (e.g. speaking at a comically fast or slow pace).

Your language choices need to be tailored for your specific audience. Think about the two scenarios just described. The following diagram shows the different language choices you would make in each.

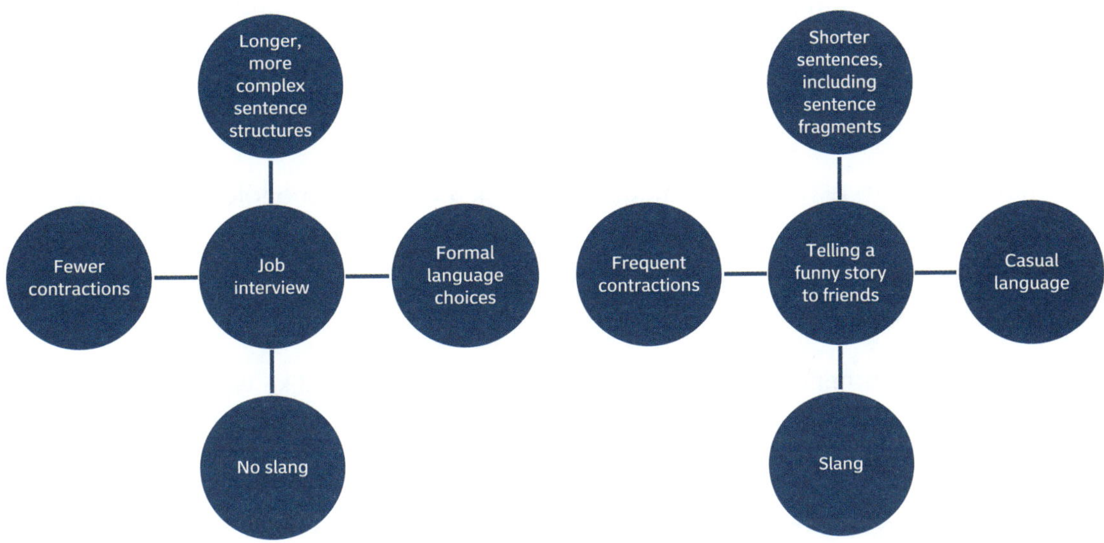

The language you choose varies depending on the situation.

Activity 7.1.5

1 **Match the language descriptions on the right to the audience and purpose they suit best on the left.**

Telling a story to a group of preschool children	A mix of formal and informal language, varied sentence structures, some slang and contractions, a friendly tone
Persuading a teacher to give you an extension on an assignment	Mostly formal language, a respectful tone, varied sentence structures
Explaining to a grandparent how to use a social media app	Simple vocabulary choices, short sentences, an enthusiastic tone, animated delivery

2 **Write the opening sentence of a speech for each of the following audiences and purposes, using appropriate language.**

a You're giving an oral presentation to your class explaining your opinion on a major theme in a novel.

b You're having a conversation with a friend about a film you both saw, which you thought was great but which they disliked.

c You want to persuade the leaders at your school to change the canteen menu to include more healthy options.

7.2 Delivering your own structured spoken texts

A well-structured spoken text is a very effective way to present information and communicate with an audience. Being able to create and present a text like this is a life skill. From presenting a team's best-and-fairest award at the end of a season, to delivering a speech at a wedding, to presenting at a conference or pitching an idea at work, there are many times in life when people need to say the right words in the right order and in the right way.

Although spoken texts can be imaginative (e.g. a dramatic monologue), formal spoken texts are generally informative or persuasive. As with written texts, your speech needs to have a clear structure. This means having an introduction, a middle and a conclusion, and a logical, clear sequence of ideas.

Because your audience can't read back over your words (unlike with a written text), you need to shape your content and delivery to help the listener understand and absorb your message. Keep the following points in mind:

- **Start with an engaging opening:** Get your audience's attention from the beginning; you could use an anecdote, present an amazing fact or just relate your topic to their everyday lives.
- **Keep most sentences short and use mainly simple or compound sentences:** (See Section 2.1 on pages 33–5 for sentence types.) Using a lot of long, complex sentences will make it hard for your listeners to follow your thoughts.
- **Use signposting words:** Words and phrases like 'first', 'second', 'as a result', 'the following reasons', 'in conclusion' and 'finally' will help your listener understand your reasoning and the connections between ideas.
- **Use repetition and rhetorical questions:** Repetition helps your audience retain information and reinforces important points, while rhetorical questions (sometimes followed by a pause) encourage your audience to reflect. Use these sparingly; they will lose their impact if overused.
- **Use the language level (or register) appropriate to your audience and context:** A conversational style might work well with a group of your peers, but formal language is better suited to presentations for assessments or official occasions.

Activity 7.2.1

Answer these questions for a spoken text you're preparing.

1 What is the topic of your text?

2 What is your purpose (e.g. to explain, to persuade)?

3 What is the main point or message you would like your audience to remember?

4 What is an attention-grabbing way you could start your text?

5 Write down a question you could ask your audience to get them interested in the topic or see its relevance to their lives.

Features of voice

The way you use your voice when speaking to an audience has a big impact on how effective your text will be. Table 7.4 summarises the main features of voice and some of their possible effects.

Table 7.4: The main features of voice and some possible effects

Feature	Explanation	Possible effects
Pace	How quickly you speak	• A faster pace can create a cumulative effect (e.g. when listing reasons). • A slower pace can be used when emphasising certain points or words.
Pauses	Breaks in the flow of your speech	• Pausing immediately after stating an important point gives listeners time to consider what has been said. • Pauses can help listeners recall what was said.
Pitch	How high or low your voice is	• A lower pitch can suggest seriousness or importance. • A higher pitch (or a rising pitch) can signal that a question is being asked, or show a speaker's uncertainty or exasperation.
Rhythm	A strong, regular repeated pattern of sounds and stresses	• A steady rhythm can convey confidence and certainty. • The rhythm can enhance the flow of words and ideas.
Tone	The mood or feeling created by word choices and delivery	• Tone helps to convey the speaker's attitude to the subject matter. • The speaker can use the tone of their voice (as well as the tone of the words) to encourage the audience to share their attitudes or feelings (e.g. an enthusiastic tone might elicit optimistic feelings).
Volume	How loudly or softly you're speaking	• Speaking softly can encourage your audience to think carefully about what you're saying. • A louder voice can be used for emphasis or to convey strong emotion.

Activity 7.2.2

1 What do you think your strengths are in speaking to a group?

2 List three things about speaking to a group that you would like to improve. You can use the features in Table 7.4 or refer to other features (e.g. speaking clearly, pronunciation, breathing).

3 How do you think you could improve the aspects of spoken delivery you identified in Question 2?

Multimodal or digital elements

You might be able to use audio, visual or audiovisual elements as part of your spoken text. These can add to the impact of your text by presenting complex information visually or summarising key points. However, don't let these elements dominate your presentation, as you could lose the connection you create with your audience.

- **Slides** should have minimal text. Use bullet points and summarise the essential information. If your audience has to focus on reading the slide, they won't be listening to you.
- **Graphs and charts** are good inclusions on slides – they provide a 'snapshot' of data and show overall patterns.
- You might incorporate a **short video**, which can convey a lot of information in a short time. Make sure it is clearly relevant and refer to it in your spoken text.

Providing feedback

Receiving and giving feedback to a peer is an excellent way to improve your spoken texts. Practising in front of a peer helps you to prepare for the 'real thing' and their feedback lets you know how you're likely to be perceived by your audience. You can use this feedback to make adjustments to your content as well as to your delivery.

Giving feedback to a peer not only helps them, it also helps you because you'll be thinking about the same aspects of your own spoken text. Use Table 7.5 as the basis for giving feedback on your peer's delivery. Remember to give positive feedback as well as constructive criticism!

Table 7.5: Feedback rubric

Category	Excellent	Average	Needs work
Voice	• Pace is fast enough to be engaging but slow enough so the listener can understand every word • Volume varies appropriately to help emphasise specific points	• Pace is a bit fast or slow • Volume is too loud or too quiet at times	• Pace is so fast it's hard to understand the words / so slow that it's hard to connect the ideas • It's hard to hear due to being too quiet / hard to listen due to being too loud
Pauses	• Pauses help to divide the main points	• There are too few/ many pauses and they interrupt the flow of ideas	• There are no pauses and points all run together • Pauses are much too long, making things disjointed
Eye contact	• Makes eye contact regularly and comfortably	• Makes a little eye contact	• Does not make eye contact
Body language	• Uses appropriate and natural hand gestures to emphasise points	• Uses some hand gestures but they seem a bit awkward	• Does not use hand gestures

Activity 7.2.3

Present your spoken text to a peer. Ask them to place ticks in the cells of Table 7.5 to show how well you are using your voice and body language. Discuss the reasons why they selected particular cells and how you might move from the 'Average' or 'Needs work' cells into the 'Excellent' cells.

Repeat the exercise, with your peer presenting and you providing the feedback.

CHAPTER 8

Word knowledge – rules, guides and patterns

English spelling has a lot of quirks. But there is a lot you can learn to make it easier, such as:

- base words, prefixes and suffixes
- borrowed words from other languages
- spelling rules.

8.1 Understanding base words, prefixes and suffixes

Base words are the core of words: they carry the essential meaning of the word, and cannot be broken down into other meaningful parts. For example, in the word 'dancer', 'dance' is the base word and '–er' has been added to the end to change the word's meaning to 'a person who dances'.

'–er' is an example of a suffix. **Prefixes** and **suffixes** are groups of letters you can add to a word to change its meaning.

Key terms

base word: the essential part of a word that can't be broken down any further and has no prefix or suffix

prefix: a combination of letters that goes at the start of a word and can change the word's meaning

suffix: a combination of letters that goes at the end of a word and can change the word's meaning

Prefixes

A **prefix** goes at the *start* of a word. For example, in the word 'unhappy', the prefix is 'un–'. Table 8.1 lists some common prefixes, what they mean and some words they appear in.

Table 8.1: Common prefixes

Prefix	Meaning	Examples
im–	not	**im**perfect, **im**mature
in–	not or inside	**in**active, **in**land
un–	not	**un**sure, **un**true
non–	not	**non**sense, **non**stop
dis–	not, away	**dis**like, **dis**miss
re–	again	**re**read, **re**write
de–	undo, remove	**de**activate, **de**-ice
mis–	wrong	**mis**read, **mis**step
pre–	before	**pre**-teen, **pre**-season

Fun fact

The word 'prefix' itself has a prefix: 'pre–'. Since 'pre–' means 'before', this can help you remember that a prefix goes *before* the rest of the word.

Activity 8.1.1

1 **Choose three prefixes from Table 8.1. Write down two other examples of words that use each prefix. Use a dictionary if you're struggling to think of words.**

2 **For two of the words you found, explain how the prefixes affect each word's meaning.**

Suffixes

A **suffix** goes at the *end* of a word. For example, the word 'clueless' has the suffix '–less'. Table 8.2 lists some common suffixes, their meaning and examples.

Table 8.2: Common suffixes

Suffix	Meaning	Example	Example meaning
–ship	state of being, position, skill	kingship	the state of being king
–ify	to make or become	solidify	to become solid
–able/ible	able to be	walkable	able to be walked

(continued)

Table 8.2: Common suffixes (continued)

Suffix	Meaning	Example	Example meaning
–er/–or	someone who or something that	gardener	someone who gardens
–ly	in a certain way	quickly	in a quick way
–y	having	rainy	having rain
–less	without	hopeless	without hope

Suffix spelling changes

Often, when you add a suffix you also need to change the spelling of the word, as shown in Table 8.3.

Table 8.3: Common suffix spelling changes

Change	Example
For many words ending in –y, a suffix will change that letter to an –i.	beauty + –ful = beautiful
If a suffix beginning with a vowel is added to a word ending in –e, the –e will often disappear.	time + –ing = timing
If the suffix starts with 'e', only one 'e' is included.	time + –er = timer
If a suffix beginning with a consonant is added to a word ending in '–e', the '–e' remains.	time + –less = timeless

Sometimes, the sound of a word changes when a suffix is added. For example, when you add '–ion' to 'promote' to make 'promotion', there is no longer a 't' sound but a 'sh' sound. The suffixes '–tion', '–cian' and '–sion' all make the same sound: 'shun'.

Some suffixes not only change the meaning of a word, but also change the type of word. For example, the verb 'write' becomes the noun 'writer' when you add the suffix '–er'.

Suffixes can also help change the tense of a word. Remember learning about verb tense in Chapter 2? '–ing' and '–ed' are also suffixes, like in 'I was walk**ing**' or 'I walk**ed**'.

Activity 8.1.2

1 **Think of two other suffixes you know that have not been mentioned in this chapter, and give two example words for each. What do you think these suffixes might mean? Look in a dictionary or search online to check whether your theory is right.**

2 Combine each word and suffix pair below to create a new word, and give your own definition of the word's meaning. Be careful to spell the new words correctly, as some will be spelled differently when a suffix is added.

- a care + er
- b love + less
- c friend + ship
- d tense + ion
- e happy + ness

8.2 Understanding the origins of words

English hasn't always looked exactly the way it does now. It has changed over hundreds of years, including by borrowing words from other languages such as **Greek** and **Latin**.

New English words were also often made by using **root words** from Greek and Latin. Understanding what these root words mean can help you piece together the meaning of the English words they form.

Table 8.4 lists some Greek and Latin root words and shows how they are used in English words.

Table 8.4: Examples of Greek and Latin roots

Root	Language	Root meaning	Example	Meaning in English
omni	Latin	all	omnivorous	eats **all** kind of food
audi	Latin	to hear	audible	can be **heard**
bio	Greek	life	biography	the written story of someone's **life**
graph	Greek	writing	biography	the **written** story of someone's life
geo	Greek	Earth	geology	the study of **Earth**

Not all English words come from Greek and Latin. Many were borrowed from French (which is related to Latin), and many have remained from older versions of English. English is related to German, so many older English words look like German words. For example, the English word 'hound' and the German word 'hund' both mean 'dog'.

Activity 8.2.1

1 **Think about the word 'television'. The Greek root word 'tele' means 'distant' or 'far'. Knowing this, explain why you think 'television' includes that root word. What do 'tele' + 'vision' mean together?**

2 **Choose one of the root words in Table 8.4. Find another word that contains this root word and write down that word's definition. Why do you think the root is used in your word? How does the root help explain the meaning of the word?**

8.3 Spelling rules to help you

English has lots of words that seem complicated to spell, but once you learn their **spelling rules** you'll find spelling them correctly much easier!

Plurals

Plural means more than one of something. To make a noun plural, usually you add one of the following suffixes:

- '–s'
- '–es'.

Key term

plural: the form of a noun when there is more one of it (e.g. houses, children)

Table 8.5 shows some of the rules for plurals.

Table 8.5: Plural rules

Rule	Examples and exceptions
–s is the most common plural suffix.	dogs, stars
–es is used when a noun ends in s, ss, sh, ch, x or z (hissing, buzzing or shushing sounds).	aliases, losses, crashes, matches, fixes, quizzes
Words that end with a consonant + o often take the –es ending.	potatoes, tomatoes (example of an exception: patios)
For many nouns ending in a consonant + y, the y will turn into an i and the –es suffix is added.	buddy → buddies
Words that end with a vowel + y (in contrast to consonant + y, as per above) usually just take the –s suffix and have no spelling changes.	monkey → monkeys
For some nouns ending in f or fe, the f changes to v and the –es suffix is added.	half → halves (example of exceptions: roofs and safes)

As you can see, when you add a plural suffix, often the spelling of the word also has to change in other ways. Note that plurals have lots of exceptions!

Fun fact

English spelling used to look very different! Hundreds of years ago, before dictionaries allowed people to agree on the spelling of words, different words often had lots of different possible spellings. People would even spell their own names in varying ways!

Aside from '-s' and '-es', there are also irregular ways to form a plural that are less common:

- the suffix '-en' (e.g. oxen, children)
- changing a vowel in the middle of the word (e.g. goose → geese)
- not changing at all (e.g. sheep).

Some of the most common words have irregular plural forms, so even though most words do not form a plural in this way, it's important to memorise them.

Table 8.6: Some common words with irregular plural forms

Singular	Plural	Singular	Plural
child	children	mouse	mice
foot	feet	sheep	sheep
goose	geese	tooth	teeth
man	men	woman	women

Remember not to use apostrophes when spelling plural words! This is a common mistake.

Key understanding

English has a lot of different ways to form the plural, so it's important to learn the rules and exceptions. When you're unsure how to spell a plural, the best way to find out is to check a dictionary.

Activity 8.3.1

What is the plural form of each of the following words?

- a book
- b fish
- c tree
- d wolf
- e cavity
- f donkey
- g array

Other spelling rules

Double letters

A word that ends with a *short* vowel and a consonant often has that consonant doubled when a suffix that starts with a vowel is added.

Table 8.7: Some words with double letters

Word that ends with a short vowel + consonant	Suffix that starts with a vowel	Final word
fit	–er	fi**tt**er
clap	–ing	cla**pp**ing
bug	–ed	bu**gg**ed

This is unlike words that end with a *long* vowel and a consonant. These do not have that consonant doubled. For example:

sleep + ing = slee**p**ing rain + ed = rai**n**ed

Understanding short and long vowels

Short vowels are quick sounds that do not sound like their letter name; for example, the 'a' in cat or the 'o' in dog.

Long vowels are pronounced like their letter name and are typically held longer. They can occur in words where the vowel is at the end or in syllables with a silent 'e' at the end. Examples of long vowel sounds include 'a' as in as in 'make' or the 'o' at the end of 'piano'.

'ough'

The combination of letters 'ough' has many different pronunciations in English, including:

'uff' (e.g. enough) 'off' (e.g. cough) 'oo' (e.g. through)

'oh' (e.g. though) 'ow' (e.g. drought)

It's also important to learn the different spellings that can give the sound 'awt':

'aught' (e.g. caught) 'ought' (e.g. bought)

Silent letters

Words often include **silent letters**. These are letters that we don't say aloud.

There are some combinations of letters where one letter is frequently silent. Some of these are included in Table 8.8.

Table 8.8: Words with silent letters

Letter combination	Silent letter	Examples
kn	k	knee, knight (be careful not to confuse this with night)
mb	b	lamb, climb
wr	r	write, wrestle
wh	h	white, what
wh	w	who, whom
sc	c	science, scent

Like many English spelling rules, there are exceptions to these.

One reason why one of these combinations might *not* contain a silent letter is because the word is a compound word. This means it's made of two separate words joined together. For example:

ham + burger = hamburger

In this example, the 'b' is pronounced, unlike in other words with 'mb' where the 'b' is silent. The two original words have retained their pronunciation in the new compound word.

Activity 8.3.2

1 Underline the silent letter in the following words.

wrench why descent knack

2 Which of the following words double their final consonant when the suffix '–ing' is added?

flap peek pit flit float stop

Literacy and technology

9.1 Understanding digital literacy

The combination of literacy and technology is often called **digital literacy**. Digital literacy means the ability to navigate the digital world using your reading, writing and technical skills, as well as **critical thinking**. It means using technology – like smartphones, computers and more – to find, evaluate and communicate information, including material supplied by **artificial intelligence**.

Key terms

digital literacy: the ability to navigate the digital world using reading, writing, technical and critical thinking skills

critical thinking: the ability to analyse information to evaluate it; identifying credible sources, evaluating arguments and assessing other viewpoints

artificial intelligence: computer systems that can perform tasks or produce information by applying machine learning techniques to large collections of data

Communicative technologies and the written word

The rise of digital technologies like text (SMS), email, direct messages and short-form video have opened up a whole new world of communication. For example, digital communication has changed the way we write. Text messages are often short, straight to the point and may contain internet slang, **GIFs** or **emojis**. Emails, meanwhile, tend to be used in professional settings so are more formal in their language and respectful in tone.

Key terms

GIF: an image file that is usually animated on a soundless loop

emoji: a small digital image used to express an idea or emotion

Think about it

Without using emojis or GIFs, how else can you convey tone in written language? If you use italics, bolding or capital letters, what kind of effect might they have?

What emojis or GIFs could you use in place of italics, bolding or capital letters? Is their effect different from just using text?

Activity 9.1.1

1 Read the following sentences and identify what type of digital communication they are – email or text message.

   a Check out this sunset – so wish you were here with us ☹

   b Thank you for reaching out. I am available for a meeting at that time.

   c Hey Ma, I should be home for dinner ♡

   d Hello students. Please check the updated assignment submission time.

Emojis are another way to add meaning in communication.

2 Read the following scenario.

> The bus is running late, delayed by heavy traffic and the wild weather. Two people huddle at the stop, cowering under umbrellas and hunched inside raincoats. Their eyes scan the road, hope rising when the bus's headlights appear. But rather than stop, it drives straight past, leaving them groaning and muttering in its wake.

   Imagine you're one of the characters in this scenario. Explain what has happened in a different way for each communication method and audience below:

   a an email to a teacher

   b a message to your friends

   c a text to your parents.

3 Working in pairs or small groups, compare your responses. Discuss how you developed them and any differences.

Analysing interactive elements

The beauty of digital forms of text is that we can interact with them. When something is in hard copy, we can read it, touch it or write on it, but there isn't much more we can do with it. However, digital texts, such as **multimodal** news articles or digital magazines, let us do and see more. The following are some common elements in digital forms that are in addition to the text.

- **Embedded links:** These are links you can click on within a web page that lead to other web pages. These can contain articles, social media posts or explanations for jargon that may not be well known.
- **Videos:** Many news articles now include videos. These can be a clip of a related news report, footage connected to the article's topic or even an advertisement.
- **Images:** Images often accompany hard copy articles too, but online you are likely to find multiple images throughout an article.

- **Advertisements:** Advertisements often surround articles, or pop up while you are reading. In addition, advertisers are sometime sneaky – a sponsored post may only include a small hashtag to let you know it's actually an ad, or an article is actually an advertorial: text that looks like the news outlet's normal content but is a paid promotion.

Key term

multimodal: characterised by several different modes; in English, usually refers to combining text with interactive or audiovisual elements

A less obvious effect of digital publishing is shorter articles. When you're online, there are so many things demanding your attention and studies show it is more difficult to read long paragraphs digitally. Additionally, videos and images published with articles can give a lot of information in a compressed space. As a result, online articles often get to the point faster and may not go into a topic in as much depth as a print article.

Think about it

When reading online, do you read the whole text? Or do you skim read it quickly to get the most important parts? Why or why don't you do this?

Next time you're tempted to skim read an article online, try to take your time instead and see if it makes a difference in your understanding.

9.2 Increasing your media literacy

With the rise of the internet and social media, news has shifted from just appearing on our television or in a newspaper. In fact, people are likely to get more of their news from digital sources than from anywhere else!

If you regularly read, watch or listen to the news, you likely know what kind of things tend to get covered – politics, world events, crime and the weather, for instance. Good news stories are often included to counter all the negative stories we see, but these don't often go **viral**.

Key term

viral: something that is circulated rapidly on the internet, such as a story, video or meme

Several factors make news attention-grabbing and more likely to go viral, such as catchy headlines, accompanying images or videos, unusual events or a relationship to current events. However, one of the biggest reasons information goes viral is due to outrage. Many technology companies amplify material that is meant to make the consumer angry, frightened or upset, as they are much more likely to share it than more everyday news reports.

This is another reason you need to think critically when reading or watching digital texts. One of the best ways to assess digital material is by applying the CRAAP test, below.

People are more likely to get their news from digital sources than other media.

C	**Currency:** How recent is the information? Newer information will probably be more relevant.
R	**Relevance:** Is the information relevant to your search?
A	**Authority:** Is the information from a credible source? This gives it authority.
A	**Accuracy:** Is the information reliable and correct? Try not to take something at face value, especially if it is generated by artificial intelligence.
P	**Purpose:** Is the purpose to inform you? Or does it seem made to provoke a reaction?

Think about it

Think about an attention-grabbing media text you've seen recently. What made you notice it? Did it provoke an emotional response from you?

Activity 9.2.1

1. **Imagine you're interested in a new set of headphones. You see a short video post about a brand on social media, and the comments below the post are all positive. What online research could you do to verify the quality of the product? How could you apply the CRAAP test to your search?**
2. **Read the following headlines and identify what the article is about and whether you think it might go viral.**
   - a **Under the microscope: scientists hard at work**
   - b **Shocking car crash video uploaded online**
   - c **New wedding photos! Australia's it couple tie the knot**
3. **In pairs or small groups, discuss which of the headlines above you think would be most likely to go viral. Why do you think this is the case? Can you think of any other topics that could go viral?**

CHAPTER 10 Analysing language, structure and ideas

10.1 Analysing language features

Throughout this book, we've looked at different language features and how authors use them to shape meaning depending on their audience and purpose. A review of common language features is shown in Table 10.1.

When analysing language, try to think like a writer, as well as a reader. A good writer will convey their message not only through the literal meanings of the words, but also through the way they use those words – the language features and literary devices in the text.

Table 10.1: Review of common language features and literary devices

Feature	Examples
Descriptive devices	Descriptive language and sensory imagery
Figurative language	Alliteration, assonance, idiom, juxtaposition, metaphor, personification, simile, symbolism
Persuasive devices (also called **rhetorical** devices)	Anecdote, appeal to fear, call to action, emotive language, **hyperbole**, inclusive language, proposition, repetition, rhetorical questions, rule of three
Poetic devices	Alliteration, assonance, onomatopoeia, repetition, rhyme and rhythm, plus other kinds of figurative language
Vocabulary devices	Formal and informal language, jargon, slang, specialised language, vocabulary choices, plus **modality** and general choices of nouns, verbs, adverbs and adjectives
Auditory features (multimodal texts)	Background music, sound effects, spoken dialogue
Visual features (multimodal texts)	Angles, colours, framing, lighting, shot size (close-up, medium shot etc.)

Note: There are many more language features and literary devices, so many that it can be overwhelming! Learn the common ones, then build your understanding as you progress through English in high school.

Key terms

rhetoric: the art of writing or speaking to persuade or argue

hyperbole: the use of exaggeration to persuade or provoke (e.g. 'We've tried this *millions* of times')

modality: a language feature used to express possibility, probability, obligation or permission; includes modal verbs (e.g. can), adverbs (e.g. possibly), adjectives (e.g. likely) and nouns (e.g. necessity)

Understanding modal verbs

Modal verbs are used to change the meaning of other verbs in a sentence. The main modal verbs include can, could, may, might, must, shall, should, will and would.

The examples below show how modal verbs modify what a sentence means.

- Isaac **may** have done his homework. (It's possible he's done it.)
- Isaac **should** have done his homework. (It's probable he's done it, but not certain.)
- Isaac **must** do his homework. (He has an obligation to do it.)
- Isaac asked, '**May** I do my homework now?' (He's asking for permission to do it.)

Activity 10.1.1

Look over one of the texts in this book or a page from a text you're studying for school. Underline the language features and literary devices you can identify.

How to analyse the relationship between language features, audience and purpose

When you analyse any language feature, you should:

1. identify the language feature
2. describe its purpose or meaning
3. consider its effect on the audience (i.e. What does this feature make the audience think or feel?).

Let's analyse the persuasive language features used in the letter to the editor in Table 10.2.

Table 10.2: Example of persuasive writing

Why cat curfews must be introduced	Contention*
I sigh as I look on the dead body of another native bird. This is the third one I have found this year. In every case, it has been killed overnight by my neighbour's cat, who is allowed to roam freely.	Anecdote
This tragic bird death is not the fault of the cat. It is doing what comes naturally to it – the animal's instinct is to hunt, especially at night.	Emotive language
It is the owners who must change their behaviour. Cats must be kept inside from 7 pm to 7 am.	Call to action
This timeframe is when many Australian native animals are most active, and when they are most vulnerable to attack. Research says domestic cats kill about 252 million mammals each year – and that count doesn't even include bird life! Why must this destruction continue so needlessly?	Rhetorical question
A cat curfew would also help the cats themselves. They are less likely to be hit by cars and less likely to get into destructive fights with one another.	Repetition
I call on the local council to implement a cat curfew as soon as possible. Save wildlife, protect cats and help neighbours get along. Melina Matarazzo	Rule of three

*As discussed in Chapter 4, the contention is the main argument.

Table 10.3 shows how to analyse the letter's written language features and literary devices.

Table 10.3: Written language features in the letter 'Why cat curfews must be introduced'

Identify the feature	Analyse the purpose of the feature	Consider the effect of the feature on the audience
Anecdote	To get the reader's attention with a dramatic story	Carries weight with readers because it's a 'true story'
Emotive language	To evoke an emotional rather than rational response	Leads the audience to share the writer's feelings on the subject
Call to action	To tell the audience what needs to be done to address the issue	Positions the audience to feel they want to take action
Rhetorical question	To engage the audience by addressing them directly	Positions readers to agree with the writer by assuming their answer will be the same as the implied one

(continued)

Table 10.3: Written language features in the letter 'Why cat curfews must be introduced' (continued)

Identify the feature	Analyse the purpose of the feature	Consider the effect of the feature on the audience
Repetition	to capture attention and make a point in a memorable way	Adds emphasis and gives the audience a sense of the writer's conviction
Rule of three	To add emphasis to a point, capturing the audience's attention	Creates a sense of completeness, making content easy to remember

For another example, we can analyse the visual features in the following advertisement (Table 10.4).

Table 10.4: Visual features in the 'Escapade by Eduardo Rodriguez' advertisement

Identify the feature	Analyse the purpose of the feature	Consider the effect of the feature on the audience
Framing and camera angle	Showing the perfume straight on and close-up makes it the central focus.	The viewer's attention is grabbed immediately as the eye is drawn to the central image.
Colours	Bright, pastel colours are meant to evoke being in a sunny location (reinforced by the palm leaf and water).	Someone who wants a holiday but can't afford it or doesn't have time may be tempted to buy the perfume instead.
Text	The word 'Escapade' and the tag line 'Take yourself on an adventure' evoke the idea of getting away from it all. 'By Eduardo Rodriguez' gives a personal, almost handmade quality to the perfume.	The viewer associates the perfume with going on a holiday or an adventure. Eduardo Rodriguez may be a celebrity or fashion designer the viewer admires, influencing their desire to buy the product.

(continued)

Table 10.4: Visual features in the 'Escapade by Eduardo Rodriguez' advertisement (continued)

Identify the feature	Analyse the purpose of the feature	Consider the effect of the feature on the audience
Lighting	The advertisement is clearly lit to display the product. The 'lens flare' (the two yellow circles reflecting off the bottle) implies that the sun is reflecting off the bottle and hitting the camera.	The idea of being in a sunny destination reinforces the theme of going on an 'escapade', encouraging the viewer to want to share this experience and buy the perfume.

Activity 10.1.2

1. **In your notebook, create a table similar to Table 10.3. Analyse three language features in an extract from this book, or one you're studying in class.**
2. **The perfume advertisement looks to be targeting people who want to escape from their everyday life. Write three sentences justifying why this is the target audience for the advertisement.**
3. **Who do you think is the target audience for the letter to the editor? Is it just the local council? Write three sentences justifying your answer.**

10.2 How to structure ideas

In Chapter 1 we looked at structure in a simple way – headings and chapters, and signalling before, next and finally. But we can take our understanding further. Table 10.5 details some structures you can use to guide your writing. These structures are especially useful when writing informative or persuasive essays.

Table 10.5: Ways to structure ideas

Text structure	Explanation
Taxonomy	A taxonomy is a way of classifying or organising things. Usually, the most important thing is placed first and the least important thing last. This is one way to plan and organise ideas for a persuasive text. You might list all your ideas in a taxonomy from the strongest idea to the weakest, and then select the top three.
Cause and effect	A cause-and-effect structure outlines the causes of a problem and then discusses each of the effects. For example, outlining multiple causes of global warming and then exploring their possible consequences.
Problem and solution	A problem-and-solution structure states a problem and then outlines one or more solutions to that problem. For example, identifying screen time as a leading cause of declining mental health in teenagers and then explaining how this problem might be solved in the future.

(continued)

Table 10.5: Ways to structure ideas (continued)

Text structure	Explanation
Extended metaphor	A single metaphor (a description of one thing as if it is another) can stretch over multiple lines or a whole text. For example, a persuasive text might present racism as a disease and then return to this metaphor at different points throughout the text.
Chronology	Structuring a text using chronology means ordering facts in temporal (time) order. For example, you might be explaining the chain of events that has caused a native animal to become more endangered over time.
Compare and contrast	Texts that use this structure show the similarities and differences between two or more things. Texts begin by introducing the things to be compared, then explain the ways they are similar or different.

The following is an extract from a cause-and-effect essay looking at how First Nations organisations are increasing awareness of First Nations languages and the effects of their efforts.

> **Australian languages and visibility**
>
> By Felicity Meakins, ARC Research Fellow (DECRA) in Linguistics, The University of Queensland
>
> [First Nations] languages suffer from a lack of visibility, but some have become better known because Indigenous organisations have been increasing our awareness of them.
>
> For example, one of the reasons that many Australians have heard of Warlpiri is due to the popularity of [television show] *Bush Mechanics* in the early 2000s, which was filmed in Warlpiri.
>
> The profile of Yolngu Matha was also raised with the release of *Ten Canoes* in 2006. It is one of the first feature films to make extensive use of an Australian language.
>
> The use of language in the performing arts and media has done a lot to raise the profile of Indigenous languages. Gumbaynggirr, a NSW language, enjoyed a moment in the spotlight in 2009 when singer-songwriter Emma Donovan released 'Ngarraanga (Remember)', which went on to win Donovan Best Female Artist and Best R&B Single at the 2009 BUMP Awards.
>
> Well-known lawyer and land rights activist Noel Pearson has also done much to promote his language, Guguu Yimithirr, in political commentary.
>
> **Get to know the language of your local area**
>
> The visibility of Australian languages in public space is on the rise. In many parts of the country, signage now greets the visitor. For example, 'Welcome to Ngunnawal' signs can be found at entry points into the ACT and surrounds.
>
> Signage is powerful. In the past it was common for interpretive signage in national parks and other public spaces to display statements such as 'this word is from Aboriginal'.

Now there are increasing examples of signage that name the language of the region, for example Gathang signs at the Great Lakes campus of TAFE in NSW, and the Wurundjeri Stories Indigenous Signage Trail in Warrandyte State Park in Victoria.

Probably the Australian capital that has done the most to increase awareness of their local language is Adelaide. As well as the extensive use of Kaurna place names in signage, the solar-powered buses have been called Tindo, which is the Kaurna word for sun. Nowadays it is hard to miss the fact that Adelaide is located on Kaurna country.

Most of the language projects that have been increasing the visibility of Australian languages are instigated by Indigenous-run language centres. Examples include Kaurna Warra Pintyanthi at Adelaide University, The Murrbay Aboriginal Language and Culture Co-op in Nambucca Heads and the Victorian Aboriginal Corporation for Languages in Melbourne. …

For Indigenous people wanting to reconnect with their languages or non-Indigenous language-learning enthusiasts, many universities now offer Indigenous-led language learning and awareness courses and activities. For example, Charles Darwin University provides courses in Yolngu Matha.

Pitjantjatjara can be learnt at the University of South Australia. Other languages offered through universities are Kaurna at the University of Adelaide and Gamilaraay at the University of Sydney.

It is important that we know that Australia is a nation of over 250 Australian Indigenous languages, not just one. It is also important that all Australians are able to name some of these, particularly the ones in our local areas. Increasing the visibility and awareness of Indigenous languages will help our nation understand the rich cultural pluralism that existed before the arrival of Europeans and continues today.

The Conversation, 8 May 2015

Note: Cultural pluralism means a society where many individual cultures can maintain their unique identity while coexisting and participating equally.

Activity 10.2.1

1 **What is the cause in the essay?**

2 **The essay talks about three main effects of First Nations organisations working to increase language awareness. Note down the effects. The first one has been done for you.**

Effect one: ***First Nations languages are appearing in television, film and performing arts.***

Effect two:

Effect three:

3 **What does the essay writer think is important?**

10.3 How to use comprehension strategies when analysing texts

In class, your teacher will ask you to analyse many written and audiovisual texts. Part of the process of analysing something is comprehending it. **Comprehension** means the ability to understand what a text means.

Key term

comprehension: the ability to read, hear or view something and understand what it means

You would have done some comprehension tasks in primary school – reading an article or story, then answering questions about it to show that you understood what the text was about. As you move through high school, you'll need to use more strategies to ensure you comprehend texts fully. Table 10.6 shows some of the main strategies.

Table 10.6: Comprehension strategies

Strategy	Explanation	Example
Visualising	Visualising means creating mental images as you read the text. Picturing scenes, characters or concepts will help you understand and remember the material.	When reading a story about a place, visualise the setting in as much detail as you can to help you understand how it might affect the characters.
Predicting	Predicting means making educated guesses about what will happen in a text. This engages your thinking more actively, helping with comprehension.	In a nonfiction text, you could use the title, headings and illustrations to predict what the material would be about. In a fiction text, you could try to predict the outcome based on the characters' actions early in the story.
Connecting	Connecting means relating the text to: • personal experiences (text-to-self) • other texts (text-to-text) • real-world events (text-to-world). Making connections helps deepen understanding and makes the content more relevant.	If a story discusses family, think about your own family and how they might be affected by the themes in the text. If an article discusses a protest overseas, you could connect this to a protest that happened in your town or city.

(continued)

Table 10.6: Comprehension strategies (continued)

Strategy	Explanation	Example
Summarising	Summarising means putting the main ideas and key details of a text in your own words. This helps you identify the most important information.	Read a newspaper article, then try to note down the essence of the report without including unnecessary details.
Monitoring	Monitoring means being aware of your understanding as you read. If something doesn't make sense, pause to re-read or clarify.	Self-monitor as you watch a film in class, especially if you notice your mind wandering. Note down anything you need to clarify when reading an essay.
Questioning	Asking questions includes querying the author's purpose, exploring themes and ideas, and questioning the meaning of specific paragraphs.	If an essay is trying to persuade you of something, use critical thinking to ask yourself why the author wants you to think a certain way and what techniques they are using to persuade you.
Inferring	Inferring means using clues from the text to figure out what an author is suggesting but not necessarily stating directly.	If an author describes a character grimacing and falling to the ground, you could infer that the character is in pain.

Comprehension helps you get the full picture of a text within your mind.

Think about it

Re-read the essay about First Nations languages on page 123, but this time focus on comprehension. For example, can you imagine the signage the writer talks about? This is visualisation. Can you speak a First Nations language, or do you know some words from your local language? This is a text-to-self connection.

Activity 10.3.1

1 Using a text you've worked on in class, apply three of the comprehension strategies described in Table 10.6.

2 How can you improve your comprehension of audiovisual texts? Write two sentences about which strategies you think would work best to help you with this.

How to compare texts

When we compare things, we consider the similarities and differences between them. We make comparisons all the time. For example, when watching a television show, you might compare its characters or storylines with those of other shows you've watched.

When comparing texts, you can make comparisons between the:

- audiences and purposes of the texts
- ideas, themes or issues explored in the texts
- representations of people, places and events
- perspectives or viewpoints the texts offer
- ways in which the texts use language features and literary devices
- quality, effectiveness or value of the texts overall.

For example, look at the two presentations below.

Presentation 1:

> Thank you all for gathering here today. I speak to you as the current school principal of Mawson College, and I am very concerned about the council's decision to reopen the access road behind the school.
>
> I am asking concerned students, parents and staff to support the school in disputing the council's short-sighted decision. They have not explained their reasons for the reopening, and I feel that allowing traffic on the access road poses a real danger to students. Even if there is not an accident, the increased pollution will have long-term negative effects.
>
> I propose we begin a letter-writing campaign to protest this change. I ask you all to write to your local councillor and outline the concerns we have around child safety, asking them to reverse their decision.
>
> I invite any of you who are alarmed to contact me with any questions you have about the school's safety campaign. Thank you again for your attention to this matter.

Presentation 2:

> Hi guys,
>
> Well today I'm going to unbox the new game from Brave Labs, 'World Rally 5'. I've been super excited to see what the Labs have done with this release, after the disappointment of number 4. World Rally 3 was such a blast, and I know a lot of you were cheesed off when the 4th instalment seemed to fall off a cliff in terms of playability.
>
> But having seen the trailer, Rally 5 looks like the developers are back on track. The visuals are awesome, and the gameplay looks smooth. So let's open up this pack and I'll get things going.

We can compare the two presentations using Table 10.7.

Table 10.7: Comparing different elements of texts

Element	Presentation 1	Presentation 2
Target audience	Students, parents and staff of Mawson College	Gamers generally, and more specifically those who enjoyed World Rally 3 but were disappointed by World Rally 4
Purpose of the text	To stop a road being a reopened	To review a new game
Ideas, themes or issues explored in the texts	That the road will endanger children at the school	That the last game was a disappointment, but hopefully the new game is an improvement
Representations of people, places and events	The audience is represented as concerned and alarmed. The council is represented as short-sighted.	The speaker says they are 'super excited'. The audience is described as 'cheesed-off' after the 4th game release.
Perspectives or viewpoints the texts offer	The perspective is one of anger at the council and concern for students' safety.	The perspective is one of anticipation and approval from an expert on this topic.
Language features and literary devices used	This is a formal persuasive speech – it uses an appeal to fear and a call to action, as well as formal language.	This is a casual and informative review – it describes the history of the previous game releases and the speaker's hopes for the new game.
Quality, effectiveness or value of the texts overall	This is quite a good presentation; however, the speaker could use more evidence and language features to improve its effectiveness.	This casual speech seems to connect well with its target audience. However, the speaker could provide more context for those not familiar with the game to attract more listeners.

Activity 10.3.2

1 Can you determine why the two presentations are different? Why is one formal and one informal?

2 What similarities between the presentations can you find?

3 Reread the evaluative language used in Table 1.4 on page 10 and the comparison language in Table 1.11 on page 25. Write a paragraph comparing the two presentations, using evaluative language and connectives that compare.

How to make predictions by analysing visual features

Look at the book cover for a hypothetical book, *Weird Planet*. What can you predict about the tone of the text inside? Who is the target audience for the book? Is it fiction or nonfiction?

Predicting means making educated guesses about what will happen in a text. This helps with comprehension by forcing your brain to engage with the text in new ways.

In Section 2.3 on page 42, we discussed the key elements to analyse in visual images. You can use these elements to analyse and predict what the tone of a book might be (re-read Table 2.11 on page 43 if you need a refresher).

For example, we can predict what we think the tone of the book *Weird Planet* is by analysing the cover's visual features (Table 10.8).

Table 10.8: Analysing visual features of a book cover and predicting the tone

Element	Analysis	Prediction
Subject	A weird planet. The title is written in a retro-style font and the general subject matter looks like science fiction.	While the book could be nonfiction, the title and the fantastical illustration style imply that it is fiction.
Setting	The cover shows a strange lunar landscape, with an old-fashioned rocket in the foreground.	The story will involve exploration, danger and adventure.
Background	The background is a dark sky with small stars and tentacles rising on the horizon.	The tentacles imply there's some kind of large monster lurking, waiting to do harm.
Colour	While the cover is colourful, the colours are washed-out and muted.	The colour scheme suggests a book or graphic novel targeted at teens and adults.

(continued)

Table 10.8: Analysing visual features of a book cover and predicting the tone (continued)

Element	Analysis	Prediction
Symbols	The retro art style is symbolic of the 1950s, when space-themed books and movies were popular.	It may have been written in the 1950s or be set in that time. This was when space exploration was very new, and people didn't know what to expect.
Overall prediction:	This book looks to be a science fiction novel or graphic novel for teens or adults. The tone would be one of daring adventure, with exploration and danger.	

Activity 10.3.3

Study the book cover below and then create a table, like the one shown, in your notebook to analyse the image and predict the tone of the book.

Element	Analysis	Prediction
Subject		
Setting		
Background		
Colour		
Symbols		
Overall prediction		

How to summarise key ideas

Summarising is a powerful tool when analysing texts, as the process of synthesising what you read helps your brain remember the text in more detail.

Creating a good summary is especially helpful when you're trying to understand the key ideas of an **extended text**.

Key term

extended text: a full-length novel, play, long poem, movie, speech, long-form journalistic investigation or informational text

Steps to summarise an extended text

The following list describes strategies you can use to summarise key ideas of paragraphs and chapters in a longer text. Ideally you would read or view the entire extended text once before starting to summarise it, but you may not always have time. If the text is part of an assessment, you may have to summarise as you go.

1. **Before you start, note down the author(s) and title of the text.** If you've already read it, jot down the main topic or theme, the audience and purpose, and any key people or characters.
2. **Read and summarise small sections of the text at a time.** Whether you're reading an article or a book, read one or two paragraphs at a time, depending on how difficult it is. If you're viewing audiovisual material, try to summarise it one or two scenes at a time. Working with small parts of the text will help you comprehend it more thoroughly.
3. **Highlight key words and write brief notes** as you read or watch each small section.
4. **Make sure you understand the text.** Monitor as you read so you notice when something is unclear. If you don't understand something, re-read it or look it up. If you zone out, restart the sentence or replay the audiovisual content. Reflect once you finish a section – did you understand it fully?
5. **Restate the main argument or points.** Try to write this out from memory using key words from the text. Even better, write it as if you're teaching it to a young child. Use your own words rather than copying the author's.
6. **Combine your summaries.** Look at your notes and highlights and combine them into a bigger text. Then review the summary as a whole – have you captured everything?

Key fact

It's important to remember what a summary is **not**. A summary is not just a shortened version of the text or a recount of the plot points of a story. It's using your own words to describe the main ideas and key details of a text. If you find yourself simply rewriting the text, revisit the steps above.

Activity 10.3.4

Choose an extended text you are studying in class, or the essay about First Nations language awareness on page 123. Using the steps described, summarise the text.

Creating texts

11.1 How to create texts for a specific audience

As we've learned, one of the first things a writer does when creating a text is to identify their target audience. This chapter will look at ways to create a variety of texts – including written, spoken, audio and audiovisual texts – for specific audiences to achieve particular purposes. We'll build on what you've already learned about crafting texts, such as selecting appropriate language, thinking about structure, and incorporating audio, visual and digital elements to create texts such as portfolios, presentations and scripts.

How to create a portfolio

One of the tasks you may be asked to do in English is to create a **portfolio**. It might be a project intended to showcase your own work, or you might be expected to work as a class or group to create a collection of texts by multiple people.

Key term

portfolio: in English, a compilation of your own or your class's writing, designed to showcase work and growth over time

To create your portfolio, you will need to:

1. define your audience
2. choose and organise your specific texts
3. present your material, including adding any audiovisual elements.

Defining your audience

The first step in putting together a collection of your work is to think about your audience, or your **intended audience**. What material would be best to include for that audience? How will they access the final product? How can you make it engaging and enjoyable for them to read or view? These questions should guide your decisions as you choose material to present.

Key term

intended audience: the audience you have in mind when creating a text; for example, if your teacher asks you to write a fairytale for an assessment, your audience will be your teacher, but your intended audience will be children who enjoy fairytales

Choosing and organising the texts

Often, your teacher will ask you to create a portfolio around a particular text type or for a particular purpose. For example, you may be asked to create a portfolio of your writing from throughout the year, or you may have to compile a portfolio of poems as a class.

If your task is to put together a collection of your own work, you could:

- choose the pieces that have received the highest marks or that you are especially proud of
- choose texts that showcase your development as a writer, starting with your less successful texts and ending with ones you feel demonstrate how your writing skills have improved.

If you are putting together a class portfolio, you'll have to work together to choose what to include – not always an easy task! Have everyone submit one or two pieces. Then use one of the organising principles in Table 11.1 to bring everything together.

Table 11.1: Organising principles for a collection

Organising principle	Example
By theme	Consider the themes or big ideas each text explores. Then group together texts that focus on similar themes.
By text type	Group poems in one section, stories in another, nonfiction text in a third and so on.
By genre	Group horror texts, romantic texts and so on in their own sections.
Alphabetically	Order texts alphabetically by author surname or by title.
Randomly	Use an online number generator or other randomised process to organise texts so you don't prioritise any individual or type of text.

Sometimes you may be asked to create extra texts for a portfolio. If your class is asked to create a portfolio of works about the environment, for example, you may combine some stories and poems you have already written but also write a nonfiction article about a bird from your area specifically for the portfolio.

Presenting the material

Although the text might be the main part of a portfolio or anthology, there are other visual elements to think about. Table 11.2 summarises some of these elements and the sorts of questions you should consider.

Table 11.2: Visual elements of a collection

Feature	Questions to consider
Illustrations	Will your collection include illustrations or artwork? Where will these come from? How many illustrations will you include?
Cover	Will the collection have a cover? What should it communicate? Think about your intended audience again – what will make them want to pick the book up? Will you include anything on the back?
Audiovisual features	Will your portfolio be digital? If so, will you include audiovisual features such as a recording of someone reading their poem or a video of a student discussing why they wrote a piece? If you're working as a group, someone will need to take responsibility for compiling everything and making sure it works.

You also need to think about the small-picture details of your portfolio, especially if you're creating an anthology of work that's meant to resemble a published book. Ensure your portfolio has a consistent look – for example, make sure font and font size for text and headings are consistent throughout. Also include a contents page and potentially a page acknowledging everyone's contributions. See pages iii–vi at the start of this book for ideas on how these should look.

Understanding group work

If you're creating a group portfolio, you'll need to use your interactive skills to work collaboratively with your classmates. Making decisions by taking a vote is one way to ensure everyone gets a say. You might also divide tasks up so that different people or small teams make decisions about particular aspects of the project – for example, creating a project schedule and keeping everyone on task, editing the texts, illustrating the collection, designing a front cover and so on.

Activity 11.1.1

1 **Imagine you're creating a class portfolio of writing about nature and the environment. Write three sentences about how you would pull everything together.**

2 **If the purpose of the portfolio is to raise awareness among your fellow students about protecting the environment, how would you present the material?**

How to track your progress and reflect on your work

As part of preparing a project, portfolio or presentation, your teacher may ask you to track your progress. You will need to reflect and write down what is happening as you work on the task.

You can track your entries either by date, recording your progress as you go, or by the stage in the process, with headings referring to different stages, e.g. planning, drafting, editing and so on.

Table 11.3 summarises aspects of your creative process that you might reflect on.

Table 11.3: Aspects of the creative process

Aspect	Questions to consider
Your target audience and main purpose	Who is your target audience? What might they know about your topic? What do you want them to feel, think or do after they've viewed your text or presentation? How do you intend to achieve this?
The main ideas	What will the general theme of your presentation or text be? What specific messages will you try to express? Why are these ideas important to you?
The form of your text	How will you communicate your ideas (e.g. in a story, a presentation, a series of poems, a video)? What are the main features of this form? How will you use them to achieve your purpose?
The structure of your text	What needs to be included in the beginning, middle and end of your text? Does the form you've chosen include visual and/or audio elements? How will you use these in a way that enhances what you're saying?
Your language choices	What sort of language will appeal to your target audience? Are there particular language features associated with the form you're creating?
Planning	How will you go about creating your text? How will you break the process into steps? Do you need to do research? How will you meet your deadline?
Successes and snags	Which parts of the process went smoothly? Which parts did you enjoy? What challenges did you have?

Think about it

The most important thing to remember about monitoring the stages of your work is to **be reflective.** Don't simply describe what you did – also discuss **why** you went about things that way. Consider what you learned from each stage in the process, and what you might do differently next time as result of what you've learned.

The following guidelines will help you to prepare effective notes about each stage of your creative process.

- **Write down notes after every stage** of a project, even if you've only completed a minor part of the task.

- **Record your notes as soon as possible** after you've done the work, while it's still fresh in your mind.
- **Break down the work into steps** and be specific about how you completed each one.
- **Conclude with an overall reflection** on the process as a whole. What went well? What didn't? What did you learn?

Activity 11.1.2

Read the following journal entry by Year 7 student Matilda, then answer the questions.

> **Final stage: receiving feedback on my presentation**
>
> At first I thought I'd present my analysis of the character of Auggie in *Wonder*, by JR Palacio, as a slide show. But then I decided a video would be better, so I could use sound effects and music more easily. This ended up being much more challenging than I thought it would be. I spent a lot of time trying to work out how to edit the video of my talk to add lots of special effects. But my teacher's comments were all about how I didn't use enough evidence from the text and quotations to support my view of Auggie.

1. **What organising principle is Matilda using for her journal?**
2. **What is one thing Matilda does well in her journal entry?**
3. **What is one thing she could do better?**
4. **Challenge: Rewrite the entry to improve it. (Make up any details you need to.)**

How to create a multimodal text

A multimodal presentation that combines words with visual or audio content can take different forms. You might create a slide presentation, video, web page or website, speech or a performance.

Remember that audio and visual elements should add to, not distract from, the information you're presenting. For each audio and visual element you include, ask yourself:

- Does this element convey new information that's not in the written text?
- Is this the best way to present this information?

While decorative elements such as pictures and sound effects can grab your audience's attention, remember that your main aim is to convey information or ideas. Don't spend so much time on the extras that you neglect the content of your presentation!

Understand text and slides

If your presentation involves you giving a talk accompanied by a set of slides, remember that most of your information needs to be presented orally, not as written text. The purpose of text on slides is to help your audience follow your ideas and to highlight key points. It's not possible for your audience – especially those at the back of the room – to read a lot of text, so keep slides simple and spend more time working on a clear, cohesive script for your talk.

Doing effective research

Whatever the topic of your presentation, you'll usually be doing some research and drawing on information and ideas from other people and organisations. The following steps will help you find good information and use it effectively in your presentations!

Step 1

- Make a list of all possible sources of information.

These might include the internet, your school library, your local library, individuals and organisations connected to your topic, and newspapers. Look for reliable sources, such as government websites or books and articles by experts.

Step 2

- Create a spreadsheet to record where you find each piece of information.

Record information in your own words.

Step 3

- Cite your sources. In your presentation, identify where you are drawing on others' information and ideas, and include their names.

You might do this in a reference list at the end and/or within the text of the presentation.

Activity 11.1.3

1 Imagine you're preparing a presentation about the director of a film you're studying. Place the following sources of information in order from most to least reliable. Then explain why you put them in this order.

- A biography of the director, written by a journalist
- Your friend, whose favourite film was directed by this director
- A comment on a message board by a film buff who thinks the director is overrated
- Your English teacher, who has been teaching students about the director's films for years

2 Use a slide show program to create a set of five slides on a topic of your choice.

3 **Write a journal entry explaining the choices you made about the following elements of the slide show:**
- **the text on the slides**
- **any illustrations or infographics you included**
- **any sound effects or music you used.**

How to create scripts

You've already learned about the conventions used in texts such as novels and poems. Audio and multimodal texts have their own particular features. Some audio or multimodal texts are spontaneous – that is, the speakers don't use a script. But many of these texts, such as podcasts, interviews, advertisements and vlogs, begin with a carefully planned and written script.

Conventions of scripts

Different types of scripts have different formats. For example, a film script is usually written in Courier font `like this`. Table 11.4 shows a podcast script about unusual hobbies. The annotations point out some general rules for scripts of any kind.

Table 11.4: Some examples of the general rules for writing scripts

Script	Rule
The podcast's jingle plays.	Many audio and audiovisual texts have their theme music, often played at the beginning of the show.
[There is the sound of a ball being kicked and a muffled fall. This is followed by the sound of young people laughing.]	Sound effects are described in square brackets.
KON: Hey guys, welcome to the latest episode of *Peculiar Pastimes*. Today our guest is Nhu, whose passion is bubble soccer. It's similar to regular soccer except the players wear inflatable bubbles around their bodies! So Nhu, take it away – what do we need to know about bubble soccer?	Speakers' names appear before their dialogue, usually capitalised and followed by a colon.
NHU (enthusiastically): Hi Kon, great to be here. Let me start with a bit of history about the sport. It was invented in Norway in 2011, with the first bubble soccer World Cup held in London in 2018. The sport is so much fun and also safer than a lot of competitive ball sports.	Stage directions or information about how a speaker should deliver their lines follows their name in round brackets.

Sound effects and music

Audio and audiovisual texts will usually include sound effects and music to communicate extra information and evoke emotions, like in the podcast example in Table 11.4. As with other multimodal presentations, an important rule to keep in mind is that these elements should be meaningful. They should enhance the script by providing extra detail, helping the audience to visualise something or communicating a mood or emotion.

Many slide show and video creation programs include sounds and music, but you can also download common sounds from free online sound effect libraries.

Activity 11.1.4

1 **Who do you think might be the main audience for the *Peculiar Pastimes* podcast? What makes you think this?**

2 **Suggest an additional sound effect to include in the podcast script in Table 11.4. Describe how this sound effect would enhance the podcast.**

3 **Write the script for a short advertisement to be played on the radio. Your script should include a description of the introductory music or jingle, stage directions for the speakers and at least two sound effects. Follow the conventions for scriptwriting. Advertise one of the following:**

- **a wooden pillow**
- **a mystery bus ride**
- **a celebrity perfume for dogs.**

11.2 Editing your own work

Editing is the process of improving a piece of writing to take it from the first draft to a polished text. When you **edit** your own work, you'll need look at the big picture of what you've written and ensure it's expressed clearly using correct grammar. A later step in this process is doing a final **proofread**.

This section gives you some strategies for editing your work, from improving your expression to correcting errors in grammar, spelling and punctuation.

Key terms

edit: check, correct and rewrite a text to fix errors and improve readability

proofread: the final check of a text to identify and correct errors in expression, grammar, punctuation and spelling

Levelling up your editing

Editing involves reading back over your work to check that it flows well and your ideas are expressed clearly. It's helpful to do this a day or two after you've written your first draft, so you can read it with fresh eyes.

However, you won't always have time to do this. Another good strategy is to read your work aloud, because errors like repetition and missing words will be more obvious when you're speaking and listening.

Editing your own work is an opportunity to re-examine and improve your writing.

Writing can often have common flaws or weaknesses that are easy to fix with some careful editing. The following explanations will help you identify weak spots and make changes so your writing is clearer, more fluent and more engaging for the reader.

Repetition

Repetition can be a flaw in writing when a word or phrase is used too many times. Of course, sometimes repetition is used deliberately; however, too much repetition weakens the impact of writing.

In this example, the phrase 'mix well' is repeated too often:

> Bring the butter to room temperature, then add the sugar and mix well. Add the vanilla and eggs and mix well. Next, add the flour, salt and baking powder and mix well. Finally, add the chocolate chips and mix well.

Phrase such as 'combine thoroughly' and 'beat until well mixed' can replace 'mix well', keeping the meaning but reducing unnecessary repetition.

Activity 11.2.1

Rewrite the following paragraph by replacing some of the repeated words and phrases.

> There was bright sunshine and a strong breeze blew across the field. All the players on the day found the bright sunshine difficult to deal with, and the strong breeze blew the ball off course. The best players adjusted, and the best scores on the day belonged to those who could deal with the bright sunshine and allow for the strong breeze.

Varying sentence structures to add fluency and refine ideas

The example of a recipe method also has another weakness – the same sentence structure is repeated. The result is writing that doesn't flow well and fails to connect the ideas. The repeated use of the conjunction 'and' is also a problem.

Aim to use a mix of simple, compound and complex sentences. Complex and compound-complex sentences (as discussed in Section 2.1 on page 36) enable you to add more information and clarify ideas. See how adding clauses and varying the conjunctions make the paragraph more interesting:

> Bring the butter to room temperature, but don't let it get too soft. Next, add the sugar and mix well so that all the granules are dissolved. Add the vanilla and egg, beating the mixture until it is thoroughly combined. Next, add the flour and baking powder and mix on a medium speed, being careful to avoid over-mixing as this will drive out all the air. Finally, add the chocolate chips and lightly stir them through.

Activity 11.2.2

1 The following paragraph consists entirely of simple sentences. Rewrite the sentences so there is a variety of sentence structures. You can add connectives and punctuation, and insert clauses with more detail if you like.

> Playing chess requires many skills. You must memorise a large number of moves. The ability to concentrate for long periods of time is essential. This is particularly true in tournament play. You need to be able to predict the consequences of moves before they happen. This is called visualisation. Finally, it is necessary to stay calm under pressure. Panic only leads to poor decision-making.

2 Break this very long sentence into shorter ones so it's easier to read.

> Skateboarding has only been an Olympic sport since 2021 but it is here to stay due to its enormous popularity around the world and its accessibility, since the only equipment needed is a skateboard and basic protective gear, in addition to a skatepark, which is much less expensive than venues such as indoor swimming pools and football stadiums, while the sport's athleticism, speed and creativity ensure its enduring appeal for participants and spectators alike.

Reordering sentences

Your main aim when writing a first draft is to get down all your ideas. However, when you read over your work, you might find that your ideas are a bit jumbled up. In instructional writing, such as recipes, the order is very important. Imagine if the recipe only told you right at the end that you needed to pre-heat the oven, or that you must leave the mixture to rest for a day before baking!

But all kinds of writing benefit from the sentences and paragraphs being placed in the most effective order. A common error in persuasive or informative writing is to place a paragraph's topic sentence somewhere in the middle of a paragraph, or even near the end. Sometimes this is known as 'burying the lead'. Consider the following paragraph from a news article.

> The cat miaowed plaintively as the man gently lifted it and carefully descended the ladder. The truck's ladder was extended and a firefighter climbed up, trying not to startle the terrified moggie. A cat had become stuck in one of the highest branches, which could only be reached by a very long ladder. Yesterday, a fire truck was called to a tall tree in Yellow Street.

It's difficult to follow the sequence of ideas in this paragraph for the simple reason that they are written out of chronological order. Also, the sentence that should 'lead' the paragraph is actually at the end. To help the reader make sense of this chain of events, the sentences can be reordered to follow a chronological sequence.

> Yesterday, a fire truck was called to a tall tree in Yellow Street. A cat had become stuck in one of the highest branches, which could only be reached by a very long ladder. The truck's ladder was extended and a firefighter climbed up, trying not to startle the terrified moggie. The cat miaowed plaintively as the man gently lifted it and carefully descended the ladder.

In writing that explains or instructs, sentences should be placed in a logical order and the main ideas should be placed at the start of a paragraph or section. In imaginative writing, though, you might like to create a sense of mystery by leaving out key details at the start.

Activity 11.2.3

Rewrite this paragraph so the sentences are in an order that makes sense.

> Last was Prancing Pony. In the middle of the field were Great Delight, Miss Lollipop and Highland Lad. The favourite Frogmore finished a disappointing fifth, just ahead of Good Karma. An exciting horse race took place at Green Gardens racecourse last night, when the first four horses had a photo finish. It took the stewards ten minutes to separate Awesome Archer, Brilliant Belle, Clever Command and Dashing Darcy into their places.

Adding or substituting words for impact

In most writing, authors aim to achieve a particular impact on their readers – they want to communicate more than just the basic facts. They can do this with elements such as:

- adjectives and adverbs
- words with connotations

- powerful verbs
- imagery
- figurative language.

For example, the adverbs 'plaintively', 'gently' and 'carefully' in the cat rescue article help to convey the emotion of this scene and the firefighter's attitude to the task. If we took these words out of the sentence it would still make sense and convey the facts, but it would have less impact and be less meaningful for the reader.

Powerful verbs can add a lot of interest to a piece of writing. Every sentence needs a verb, but it's easy to overuse common verbs such as 'looked' and 'walked'. By substituting these with more precise verbs such as 'peered' and 'strolled', an author can convey emotions and suggest states of mind.

Adding words for coherence

Editing can also help to make a text more coherent – that is, logical and consistent. This can be done through reordering sentences and paragraphs so ideas flow more logically. You can also add or replace connectives to show sequence, cause and effect, or similarities and differences. See Section 1.4 for more on how connectives can help your reader to see how ideas are linked and developed.

Checking grammar

There are many ways in which grammar can be incorrect. Here are three of the main errors that creep into writing.

- **Inconsistent verb tenses:** Generally, a sentence should be in past tense, present tense or future tense, not a combination of two or more tenses. The example below uses both present tense ('make') and past tense ('knocked'), which makes it hard for the reader to work out the timeline.

  I quickly make the caramel sauce but accidently knocked the saucepan onto the floor.

- **Sentence fragments:** A correct sentence has a noun and a verb – most sentence fragments lack one of these. For example, this sentence fragment lacks a verb:

  A very sticky situation.

- **Incorrect subject-verb agreement:** This arises when a singular noun is followed by a plural verb, or vice versa. In this example, the verbs should be 'explains' (singular, to go with the singular 'cookbook') and 'turn' (to go with the plural 'sauces').

  The cookbook we are using explain that caramel sauces turns into toffee quickly.

Activity 11.2.4

The following sentences have grammatical errors. Rewrite each sentence correctly.

1 **There is 52 playing cards in a traditional pack.**

2 **Which is made up of four suits: diamonds, hearts, clubs and spades.**

3 **In the early 1400s the suits are swords, clubs, cups and coins, but these were replaced in the late 1400s by the modern suits.**

4 **Playing card games are very popular and the availability of classic card games online make them even easier to play.**

Checking spelling

You learned rules to improve your spelling in Chapter 8. Here are some more things to look out for.

- **Check for homophone confusion.** It's easy to mix up words that sound alike, such as 'there', 'they're' and 'their'; 'practise' (a verb) and 'practice' (a noun); and 'compliment' (praise) and 'complement' (something that adds to or goes with something else).
- **Check for the correct use of suffixes.** Some of the most frequently misspelled words are those that have endings like '-ation', '-able', '-ible', '-ant', '-ent', '-ance' or '-ence'. Memorise the spellings of some common words with suffixes, such as descendant and independent.
- **Check for accidental phonetic spellings** – these occur when you spell a word as it sounds, which does not always lead to the correct spelling. Examples include 'contraversy' instead of 'controversy' and 'Febuary' instead of 'February'.
- **Check the spellings of words with silent letters** (e.g. '**g**nome', 'play**w**right', 'shou**l**d' and 'plum**b**er') to make sure you've included all letters.
- **Look out for spellings in US English.** Common examples include 'color' (instead of 'colour'), 'defense' (instead of 'defence') and 'practice' as a verb (instead of 'practise').

Activity 11.2.5

Identify the misspelled or misused words in these sentences and write the correct spelling.

1 **Our teem has been succesful but we are too dependant on our best player.**

2 **Defense wins matches, not offense – incredable players practice both skills equelly.**

3 **They need a tall player to compliment the existing players, because their mostly short.**

Punctuation

Don't forget the basics of punctuation such as capitals, full stops, apostrophes and plurals.

- Sentences should start with a capital letter and end with a full stop, exclamation mark or question mark.
- Apostrophes are used for possessives (e.g. 'Abdul**'s** e-scooter was very fast.'). Exception: **Its** does not use an apostrophe (e.g. 'Claudia's e-Scooter was faster than Abdul's because **its** battery was more powerful.'). It's with an apostrophe is short for 'it is'.
- Plural words ending in 's' do not take an apostrophe. If you see a sign saying 'Apple's for sale!' let the shop know they need to check their punctuation rules!

Activity 11.2.6

Rewrite the following sentences with the correct punctuation.

1 **Do you know what time the game begins.**

2 **The students basketball team won their last game of the season, but its going to be a lot harder in the final's.**

3 **Id rather be on the court from the start, but I know some players' like to come off the bench.**

Editing texts collaboratively

When more than one person (such as a writer and an editor) work on a document using word-processing software (such as Microsoft Word), the Comment feature can be used to raise queries and signal changes. This allows for the document to be sent back and forth between the collaborators and a conversation to take place within the comment boxes.

It's also possible for collaboration to be done on a 'live' document, using a platform such as Google Classroom. Collaborating this way avoids the need for the document to be emailed back and forth.

As with any form of feedback, the comments you write should be respectful and constructive. Use phrases such as 'Could you add …', 'I suggest …' and 'Could this be reworded as …' to offer suggestions. Blunt comments such as 'This doesn't make sense' or 'This is wrong' don't give your collaborator much to work with and can lead to unhelpful tension and conflict.

Curriculum correlation

The grid below shows how *Summary Guides – English 7* matches the Year 7 English curriculum requirements for your state.

Chapter	Curriculum code – Australia (includes Qld, SA and Tas)	Curriculum code – Victoria	Curriculum code – NSW	Curriculum code – Western Australia
Chapter 1 Using language to express yourself and interact with others	AC9E7LA01 AC9E7LA02 AC9E7LA03 AC9E7LA04	VC2E7LA01 VC2E7LA02 VC2E7LA03 VC2E7LA04	EN4-URB-01	WA7ELAI1 WA7ELAI2 WA7ELAT1 WA7ELAT2
Chapter 2 Using language to express your ideas	AC9E7LA05 AC9E7LA06 AC9E7LA07 AC9E7LA08 AC9E7LA09 AC9E7LE06	VC2E7LA05 VC2E7LA06 VC2E7LA07 VC2E7LA08 VC2E7LA09	EN4-URA-01	WA7ELALA1 WA7ELALA2 WA7ELALA3 WA7ELALA4 WA7ELALA5
Chapter 3 Literature and contexts	AC9E7LE01	VC2E7LE01	EN4-RVL-01 EN4-URC-01	WA7ELICO1
Chapter 4 Engaging with literature	AC9E7LE02 AC9E7LE03	VC2E7LE02 VC2E7LE03	EN4-RVL-01 EN4-URA-01 EN4-URB-01 EN4-URC-01	WA7ELIEN1 WA7ELIEN2
Chapter 5 Examining literature	AC9E7LE04 AC9E7LE05 AC9E7LE06	VC2E7LE04 VC2E7LE05	EN4-RVL-01 EN4-URB-01	WA7ELIEN1 WA7ELIEX1 WA7ELIEX2
Chapter 6 Creating your own literature	AC9E7LE07	VC2E7LE06	EN4-ECA-01	WA7ELICR1
Chapter 7 Interacting with others – speaking and listening	AC9E7LY02	VC2E7LY01 VC2E7LY02	EN4-ECA-01	WA7ELYI1 WA7ELYC2
Chapter 8 Word knowledge – rules, guides and patterns	AC9E7LY08	VC2E7LY03	EN4-ECA-01	WA7ELAW1
Chapter 9 Literacy and technology	AC9E7LY01	VC2E7LY04	EN4-URB-01 EN4-ECA-01	WA7ELYT1 WA7ELYC4
Chapter 10 Analysing language, structure and ideas	AC9E7LY03 AC9E7LY04 AC9E7LY05	VC2E7LY05 VC2E7LY06 VC2E7LY07	EN4-URA-01 EN4-ECB-01	WA7ELYA1 WA7ELYA2 WA7ELYA3
Chapter 11 Creating texts	AC9E7LY06	VC2E7LY08 VC2E7LY09	EN4-URA-01 EN4-ECA-01 EN4-ECB-01	WA7ELYC1 WA7ELYC4